Advanced Data Structures: Boost Your Programming with Complex Algorithms

A Step-by-Step Guide to Advanced Concepts in Data Structures

MIGUEL FARMER

RAFAEL SANDERS

All rights reserved

Table of Content

TABLE OF CONTENTS

INTRODUCTION

Mastering Data Structures and Algorithms: Foundations, Advanced Techniques, and Emerging Trends

In the world of modern computing, **data structures** and **algorithms** are the bedrock of efficient software design and problem-solving. From the simplest of tasks to the most complex computational challenges, the right data structure and algorithm can make a world of difference in terms of **performance**, **scalability**, and **efficiency**. Whether you're developing software, optimizing systems, or analyzing vast datasets, understanding the inner workings of data structures and algorithms is essential.

This book, *"Mastering Data Structures and Algorithms: Foundations, Advanced Techniques, and Emerging Trends"*, is crafted to guide readers through the vast and evolving landscape of these foundational concepts. The aim is to provide both a **comprehensive understanding** of traditional data structures and algorithms and a forward-looking exploration of emerging trends and techniques that are shaping the future of computing.

The Importance of Data Structures and Algorithms

Every computer program or system needs to manage data in some way. From **storing information** to **processing data, retrieving data efficiently**, and **solving complex computational problems**, the tools that manage and manipulate data—**data structures** and **algorithms**—are indispensable.

- **Data Structures** are ways of organizing and storing data so that operations such as **searching, insertion, deletion,** and **modification** can be performed efficiently.
- **Algorithms** are step-by-step procedures or formulas for solving a problem. They dictate how data is processed and manipulated within the program or system.

Efficient algorithms and well-chosen data structures enable systems to operate with higher **speed, accuracy**, and **scalability**. A small inefficiency can lead to large performance bottlenecks, especially in large-scale systems or data-heavy applications like search engines, social networks, databases, and machine learning models.

What This Book Covers

This book is structured to provide both foundational knowledge and insights into the future of **data structures** and **algorithms**. It is divided into three main sections:

1. Foundational Concepts:

The first part of the book focuses on the core principles of data structures and algorithms. It introduces the most widely-used data structures—such as arrays, linked lists, trees, heaps, and graphs—and the essential algorithms for searching, sorting, and optimizing data. With clear examples and step-by-step explanations, readers will learn how to:

- Analyze algorithm **complexity** using Big O notation.
- Choose the most appropriate **data structures** for specific problems.
- Solve fundamental problems such as searching, sorting, and graph traversal using efficient algorithms.

2. Advanced Techniques and Algorithms:

The second section dives into more **advanced data structures** and **complex algorithms**. Here, we explore:

- **Dynamic programming** and **greedy algorithms**, which provide powerful techniques for solving optimization problems.

- **Parallel algorithms** for speeding up computation on multi-core systems.
- **Distributed data structures** for scalable and resilient systems, such as **distributed hash tables (DHTs)**, **quorum-based approaches**, and **consistent hashing**.

These concepts are increasingly relevant as systems become larger, more distributed, and more complex.

3. Emerging Trends and the Future:

The final part of the book looks toward the future. With the rise of emerging technologies like **quantum computing**, **AI**, **blockchain**, and **machine learning**, data structures and algorithms are undergoing a radical transformation. We will explore:

- How **quantum computing** is influencing new data structures and algorithms.
- The role of **machine learning** in developing **AI-based data management** techniques.
- The integration of **blockchain** into modern data structures for secure, decentralized data storage and retrieval.

This section highlights how these advancements will shape the future of computing, making the book relevant not just for understanding today's technologies but also for preparing for tomorrow's innovations.

Who Should Read This Book?

This book is designed for a wide range of readers, from **beginners** to **experienced professionals**:

- **Students** studying computer science or related fields will find a solid grounding in data structures and algorithms, laying the foundation for future learning.
- **Software developers** and **engineers** can gain practical knowledge to write more efficient, scalable, and maintainable code, improving their problem-solving skills.
- **Advanced practitioners** working with **large-scale systems**, **machine learning**, **distributed systems**, or **quantum computing** will appreciate the discussions of advanced topics and emerging trends that will shape the future of technology.

Whether you are new to the subject or already have experience with data structures and algorithms, this book will deepen your understanding and equip you with the knowledge to tackle complex computational problems in the modern world.

Why This Book?

- **Clear Explanations and Examples:** Each concept is explained with detailed examples, visual aids, and step-by-step breakdowns to help readers grasp difficult topics.

- **Comprehensive Coverage:** This book doesn't just focus on the basics—it also introduces advanced topics, offering readers a holistic view of data structures and algorithms, from fundamentals to future innovations.

- **Practical Applications:** Real-world examples are woven throughout, helping readers understand how these concepts are applied in technologies like **distributed databases**, **web search**, **cloud computing**, and **AI**.

- **Looking Ahead:** The final section on emerging technologies positions the reader at the forefront of cutting-edge developments, providing insight into the future direction of data structures and algorithms.

Conclusion

"Mastering Data Structures and Algorithms: Foundations, Advanced Techniques, and Emerging Trends" serves as both a **comprehensive guide** and a **future-facing exploration** of this essential area of computer science. With the growing complexity of modern systems and the arrival of transformative technologies,

17

understanding how to design, implement, and optimize data structures and algorithms is more important than ever.

Through this book, you will not only gain a deeper understanding of classic algorithms and data structures but also be equipped with the tools and insights necessary to navigate the exciting challenges ahead. Whether you are building the next great software system, designing an AI application, or preparing for the quantum revolution, this book will help you master the algorithms that power the world of tomorrow.

CHAPTER 1

INTRODUCTION TO ADVANCED DATA STRUCTURES

In the world of computer science and software development, **data structures** form the backbone of efficient algorithms and system design. Whether it's for handling large amounts of data, improving search speed, or optimizing memory usage, the way data is organized and managed plays a crucial role in the performance and scalability of an application.

In this chapter, we will introduce the concept of **advanced data structures**, explore their importance in optimizing algorithms, and provide a preview of how this book will guide you in mastering complex algorithms through hands-on examples and real-world applications.

Overview of Data Structures and Their Importance in Programming

A **data structure** is a particular way of organizing and storing data in a computer so that it can be accessed and modified efficiently. The choice of data structure directly impacts the performance of algorithms, as different data structures are optimized for different types of operations.

For example:

- **Arrays** are ideal for sequential access and fixed-size collections.
- **Linked lists** are useful when you need to insert and delete elements efficiently.
- **Stacks and queues** are essential for managing data in specific orders (LIFO and FIFO, respectively).

At its core, a good data structure ensures that an algorithm works efficiently in terms of time and space complexity. A **well-chosen data structure** can lead to faster processing and lower memory consumption, which are crucial factors in the success of any software system.

Key Characteristics of Data Structures:

- **Time Complexity:** How long an operation takes relative to the size of the data (e.g., searching, inserting, deleting).
- **Space Complexity:** How much memory is required to store the data.
- **Operations:** The primary operations supported by a data structure (e.g., searching, inserting, deleting, updating).

As the complexity of a system increases, the need for more advanced data structures becomes clear. This is particularly true when dealing with large datasets or systems that require high performance, such as web servers, databases, and real-time processing systems.

Why Understanding Advanced Data Structures is Crucial for Optimizing Algorithms

Advanced data structures go beyond the basic constructs and provide more specialized ways to manage data efficiently. While simple data structures like arrays, lists, and stacks are suitable for small-scale problems, large-scale systems with millions of data entries require more sophisticated solutions.

The Role of Advanced Data Structures in Algorithm Optimization:

1. **Improving Algorithm Efficiency:**
   o Advanced data structures like **heaps**, **tries**, and **graphs** enable algorithms to perform tasks in **less time** (e.g., finding the shortest path, searching efficiently in a large database, or scheduling jobs).

21

- o For example, using a **hash table** can reduce search time to **O(1)**, compared to a linear search with **O(n)** time complexity.

2. **Memory Management and Utilization:**
   - o Some advanced data structures, such as **B-trees** and **segment trees**, allow for efficient storage and retrieval of data in disk-based storage systems or in-memory, making it possible to process large datasets without consuming excessive memory.

3. **Parallelism and Distributed Computing:**
   - o In distributed systems or multi-threaded environments, data structures like **disjoint sets (union-find)** and **queues** are crucial for managing tasks like network communication, concurrent processing, and maintaining data consistency across different nodes.

4. **Handling Complex Operations:**
   - o Complex operations like **range queries**, **sorting large datasets**, and **pattern matching** benefit from specialized data structures such as **segment trees** or **Trie data structures**. These structures allow algorithms to execute efficiently even under heavy load or with highly dynamic datasets.

By mastering advanced data structures, you equip yourself with the tools to write optimized, high-performance algorithms that can scale and handle real-world challenges effectively. This is why understanding how to implement and apply these structures is crucial for anyone aspiring to work with large-scale systems or tackle performance-critical applications.

A Look at Common Use Cases for Advanced Data Structures in Real-World Applications

The importance of advanced data structures becomes clear when we consider how they are used in real-world applications. Here are some examples where advanced data structures are pivotal:

1. **Databases and File Systems:**
   - o **B-trees** and **B+ trees** are widely used in database indexing systems, enabling quick search, insert, and delete operations in disk-based storage systems.
   - o **Hashing** plays a major role in implementing fast lookup operations in key-value stores like **Redis** and **HashMap** in Java.
2. **Networking and Distributed Systems:**
   - o **Disjoint-set data structures** (union-find) are used in network connectivity problems, like detecting cycles in a graph, or in distributed

23

systems for managing group membership in a dynamic network.

- o **Queues** and **priority queues** are used in networking protocols and real-time systems for scheduling tasks and managing buffers (e.g., HTTP request handling, task scheduling in operating systems).

3. **Search Engines and Autocomplete:**
    - o **Trie data structures** are widely used in search engines for implementing **autocomplete** functionality, providing quick prefix-based search in dictionaries or user search history.
    - o **Bloom filters** are used for **probabilistic** set membership testing in cases where space efficiency is essential, such as in **spam filtering** or **URL filtering** in large systems.

4. **Real-Time Systems:**
    - o **Heap-based priority queues** are used for managing scheduling tasks in real-time systems, where the goal is to allocate resources or prioritize tasks dynamically based on certain criteria (e.g., job scheduling in operating systems).
    - o **Graphs** and **network flow algorithms** are crucial in pathfinding applications, such as GPS systems or autonomous vehicle navigation.

5. **Compilers and Syntax Tree Parsing:**

   o **Trees** are used extensively in **compilers** and **interpreters** for representing **abstract syntax trees (AST)**, which are crucial in analyzing and optimizing code.

   o **Graphs** are used for optimizing program execution, such as in **data flow analysis**.

How This Book Will Guide You Through Mastering Complex Algorithms

This book is designed to demystify the complex world of advanced data structures and algorithms by breaking down intricate concepts into manageable, step-by-step explanations. Here's how we'll guide you through mastering these topics:

Step-by-Step Approach:

Each chapter will focus on a specific data structure, starting with a simple introduction, followed by in-depth discussions on its properties, implementation, time and space complexities, and practical applications. We will also provide code examples in multiple programming languages to help you see how these data structures are implemented and used in practice.

Real-World Applications:

Throughout the book, we'll integrate **real-world use cases** to demonstrate the importance of each data structure in solving problems. You'll see how different data structures are applied in areas like databases, networking, machine learning, and more.

Problem Solving and Algorithms:

The book will focus not only on theoretical knowledge but also on practical problem-solving. Each chapter will include algorithmic challenges and exercises designed to test your understanding and improve your problem-solving skills.

Advanced Techniques:

As you progress, the book will introduce advanced concepts and specialized data structures, such as **segment trees**, **Trie trees**, and **disjoint set data structures**. You'll gain expertise in how to optimize algorithms, handle large datasets, and scale your applications.

Conclusion

Understanding advanced data structures is a critical skill for any software developer or systems architect. They provide the foundation for creating efficient algorithms and scalable systems. This book is designed to take you on a journey from basic data structures to advanced concepts, helping you master complex algorithms and apply them effectively to real-world problems. By the end of this book, you will have the knowledge and skills needed to build optimized, high-performance software systems that can handle even the most demanding tasks.

This chapter serves as an introduction to the world of **advanced data structures**, emphasizing their importance and setting the stage for the detailed exploration in the subsequent chapters. Whether you're looking to optimize your algorithms, handle large-scale data, or solve complex problems, this book will help guide you through the necessary techniques and approaches.

CHAPTER 2

REVIEW OF BASIC DATA STRUCTURES

Before diving into the complexities of advanced data structures, it's essential to establish a strong foundation in the **basic data structures**. These building blocks are crucial for understanding more complex systems and algorithms. In this chapter, we will provide a quick refresher on fundamental data structures such as **arrays**, **linked lists**, **stacks**, and **queues**. We will also examine their **time** and **space complexities** and discuss how they serve as the foundation for more advanced data structures.

Brief Refresher on Basic Data Structures

1. Arrays

An **array** is a collection of elements stored at contiguous memory locations. It is one of the most fundamental data structures, providing fast access to elements through an index. Arrays are particularly efficient when the size of the collection is known in advance.

- **Properties:**
    - **Fixed Size:** The size of an array is typically fixed once it is created.
    - **Index-Based Access:** Elements can be accessed in constant time using an index.
    - **Homogeneous Elements:** Arrays store elements of the same type (e.g., integers, strings).
- **Common Operations:**
    - **Access:** Accessing an element by its index takes constant time, **O(1)**.
    - **Insert/Remove:** Inserting or removing an element at the beginning or in the middle requires shifting elements, resulting in a time complexity of **O(n)**.
    - **Insert/Remove at the end:** This operation takes **O(1)** time in the best case for dynamic arrays.
- **Use Cases:**
    - **When to use:** Arrays are ideal for situations where the size is known ahead of time and random access is needed (e.g., storing values in a table, matrix operations).
    - **Example:** Storing a list of students' grades in a class.

2. Linked Lists

A **linked list** is a linear data structure in which elements (nodes) are connected using pointers. Each node contains two parts: the data and a reference (or pointer) to the next node in the sequence.

- **Properties:**
  - o **Dynamic Size:** Linked lists allow dynamic memory allocation, meaning the size can grow or shrink during runtime.
  - o **Sequential Access:** Elements are accessed sequentially, starting from the head (first node).
  - o **No Direct Access:** Unlike arrays, linked lists do not allow direct access to elements based on an index.
- **Common Operations:**
  - o **Access:** Accessing an element requires traversing the list from the head node, which takes **O(n)** time.
  - o **Insert/Remove:** Inserting or removing an element at the head or tail of a singly linked list can be done in **O(1)** time. Inserting/removing in the middle requires traversing the list, making the time complexity **O(n)**.
- **Use Cases:**
  - o **When to use:** Linked lists are useful when the size of the collection is unknown or changes

frequently (e.g., real-time applications where elements are added or removed dynamically).

- o **Example:** Implementing a task scheduler or handling dynamic data that changes frequently.

3. Stacks

A **stack** is a linear data structure that follows the **Last In First Out (LIFO)** principle. The last element added is the first one to be removed. Stacks are often used in situations where tasks need to be performed in reverse order.

- **Properties:**
  - o **LIFO Order:** The last element pushed onto the stack is the first to be popped off.
  - o **Two Main Operations:** push (add an element) and pop (remove an element).
  - o **Auxiliary Operations:** peek (view the top element without removing it) and isEmpty (check if the stack is empty).
- **Common Operations:**
  - o **Push/Pop:** Both push and pop operations take **O(1)** time, as they involve adding or removing an element from the top of the stack.
  - o **Peek:** The peek operation also takes **O(1)** time, as it only involves accessing the top element.

31

- **Use Cases:**
    - ○ **When to use:** Stacks are used in algorithms that require a last-in, first-out structure, such as **depth-first search (DFS)**, **undo functionality** in text editors, or **function calls** in programming languages (call stack).
    - ○ **Example:** Tracking function calls in recursion or maintaining the history of visited pages in a web browser.

---

4. Queues

A **queue** is a linear data structure that follows the **First In First Out (FIFO)** principle. The first element added is the first one to be removed. Queues are typically used in scenarios where tasks need to be handled in the order they are received.

- **Properties:**
    - ○ **FIFO Order:** The first element enqueued is the first to be dequeued.
    - ○ **Two Main Operations:** `enqueue` (add an element) and `dequeue` (remove an element).
    - ○ **Auxiliary Operations:** `front` (view the front element without removing it) and `isEmpty` (check if the queue is empty).
- **Common Operations:**

32

- o **Enqueue/Dequeue:** Both enqueue and dequeue operations are **O(1)**, as elements are added or removed from the front and back of the queue, respectively.
- o **Front:** The `front` operation also takes **O(1)** time.
- **Use Cases:**
  - o **When to use:** Queues are used in scenarios where tasks or data must be processed in the order they arrive, such as in **job scheduling, print spooling,** and **network packet management.**
  - o **Example:** Managing a queue of print jobs sent to a printer or handling requests in a web server.

Time and Space Complexities of Basic Structures

When choosing a data structure for a given problem, it's essential to consider both **time complexity** (how fast operations can be performed) and **space complexity** (how much memory is used). Here is a breakdown of the most common operations for basic data structures:

Data Structure	Operation	Time Complexity	Space Complexity
Array	Access	O(1)	O(n)
	Insertion (end)	O(1)	O(n)
	Insertion (middle)	O(n)	O(n)
	Deletion (end)	O(1)	O(n)
	Deletion (middle)	O(n)	O(n)
Linked List	Access	O(n)	O(n)
	Insertion (head)	O(1)	O(n)
	Insertion (tail)	O(1) (if doubly linked)	O(n)
	Deletion (head)	O(1)	O(n)
Stack	Push	O(1)	O(n)
	Pop	O(1)	O(n)

Data Structure	Operation	Time Complexity	Space Complexity
	Peek	O(1)	O(n)
Queue	Enqueue	O(1)	O(n)
	Dequeue	O(1)	O(n)
	Front	O(1)	O(n)

- **Time Complexity:** Represents the amount of time it takes to perform an operation as the size of the data structure increases. For example, **O(n)** means that the operation takes linear time, and the execution time increases proportionally with the size of the data structure.
- **Space Complexity:** Represents the amount of memory used by the data structure. For example, an array of n elements requires **O(n)** space.

Transition from Basic to Advanced Data Structures

Once you've mastered the basics of arrays, linked lists, stacks, and queues, it's time to move on to **advanced data structures**. While the basic structures provide fundamental functionality, advanced structures are designed to handle more complex problems efficiently. For example:

- **Hash tables** allow for fast lookups with constant time complexity, offering a more efficient alternative to arrays for many types of data retrieval operations.
- **Trees** like **binary search trees (BSTs)** and **AVL trees** allow for efficient searching, insertion, and deletion while maintaining order.
- **Graphs** help model complex relationships in systems such as social networks, routing algorithms, and dependency management.

The transition to advanced data structures requires understanding the limitations and trade-offs of basic structures and then learning how to apply more sophisticated approaches to solve larger, more complex problems efficiently.

Advanced data structures are often designed to solve specific issues like:

- **Efficient searching and sorting** (e.g., AVL trees, B-trees).
- **Handling dynamic data** (e.g., splay trees, hash maps).
- **Managing large datasets in a memory-efficient way** (e.g., tries, segment trees).

- **Enabling high-performance parallelism and distributed computing** (e.g., bloom filters, disjoint-set).

This book will guide you step by step as you dive into these advanced structures, helping you understand when and how to use them effectively.

Conclusion

Understanding basic data structures is a necessary first step in becoming proficient in computer programming and algorithm design. While simple data structures like arrays, linked lists, stacks, and queues solve many problems, more advanced data structures are essential for tackling complex, large-scale problems efficiently. As we move forward in this book, we will explore these advanced structures in detail and show how they can optimize algorithms and applications, ultimately improving performance and scalability in real-world systems.

In the next chapter, we will dive into **self-balancing binary search trees**, starting with **AVL trees**, and explore their role in optimizing search, insertion, and deletion operations. Let's continue building on this foundation to unlock the power of advanced data structures!

CHAPTER 3

COMPLEXITY ANALYSIS: UNDERSTANDING BIG O NOTATION

In the world of software development, efficiency is key. While a solution to a problem might work, how well it performs under different conditions is just as important. **Algorithm efficiency** plays a critical role in determining how well a program will scale when handling larger datasets or more complex operations. To assess the efficiency of an algorithm or data structure, we need a framework that allows us to analyze **time** and **space complexity**. One of the most widely used tools for this is **Big O notation**.

In this chapter, we will break down:

- The **importance of analyzing algorithm efficiency**.
- The concepts of **time complexity** and **space complexity**, and how they guide the selection of the right data structure.
- The different types of **Big O**, **Big Ω**, and **Big Θ** notation, and what they represent.

- **Real-world examples** of complexity analysis in choosing data structures, helping you understand how to apply these concepts in practice.

The Importance of Analyzing Algorithm Efficiency

When solving a problem, **correctness** is often the primary concern. However, once a solution is working, the next key question is: **How efficient is it?** The efficiency of an algorithm or data structure can significantly impact the overall performance of a program, especially when dealing with large datasets or high-performance applications.

Why Efficiency Matters:

- **Scalability:** As the input size grows, the time and space required by an algorithm can increase dramatically. An algorithm that works fine with small inputs may become unacceptably slow or resource-intensive as the size of the data increases.
- **Resource Utilization:** Efficient algorithms minimize the use of time and memory, which directly translates into better **resource utilization** and lower operational costs.

- **User Experience:** Performance issues can degrade user experience. For example, long wait times for a web page to load or a delay in data processing due to inefficient algorithms can result in poor user satisfaction.

Therefore, understanding the efficiency of your algorithms and data structures is critical to ensuring that your program is both functional and performant.

Time Complexity, Space Complexity, and Their Role in Selecting the Right Data Structure

To understand the performance of an algorithm, we focus on two primary metrics: **time complexity** and **space complexity**.

1. Time Complexity:

Time complexity refers to the amount of time an algorithm takes to run as a function of the size of its input. It provides insight into how the execution time increases as the input size grows. Understanding time complexity helps in predicting how well an algorithm will scale with larger datasets.

- **Common Time Complexities:**
  - **O(1):** Constant time – The execution time does not depend on the size of the input.

- o **O(log n):** Logarithmic time – The execution time grows logarithmically with input size (common in binary search).
- o **O(n):** Linear time – The execution time grows linearly with input size.
- o **O(n log n):** Log-linear time – Typical for efficient sorting algorithms like Merge Sort and Quick Sort.
- o **O(n²):** Quadratic time – The execution time grows quadratically with input size (common in nested loops, such as Bubble Sort).
- o **O(2^n):** Exponential time – The execution time grows exponentially with input size (typical in brute-force approaches).

2. Space Complexity:

Space complexity measures the amount of memory an algorithm needs to run as a function of the input size. Efficient algorithms make sure they use a minimal amount of space, especially when working with large datasets.

- **Factors Influencing Space Complexity:**
  - o The amount of **extra memory** used by the algorithm (e.g., temporary variables, auxiliary data structures).

o   The **input size** and how much memory is used to store it (e.g., a list, array, or graph).

Choosing the Right Data Structure:

When designing algorithms, selecting the appropriate data structure can significantly impact time and space complexity. For instance:

- **Arrays** allow for fast access, but inserting or deleting elements requires shifting, leading to **O(n)** time complexity.
- **Hash tables** offer **O(1)** average-time complexity for search operations but require extra memory for storing key-value pairs.
- **Trees** like **AVL trees** offer **O(log n)** search times, but their space complexity may vary based on the tree structure and balance.

Selecting the right data structure is crucial to optimize the efficiency of your algorithms and ensure that they perform well under different conditions.

Big O, Big Ω, and Big Θ Notation

In algorithm analysis, we use **Big O**, **Big Ω**, and **Big Θ** notation to describe the **asymptotic behavior** of an algorithm, which refers to its performance as the input size grows toward infinity.

1. Big O Notation (O) – Worst-Case Time Complexity

- **Definition:** Big O notation describes the **upper bound** of an algorithm's running time. It represents the worst-case scenario, i.e., the maximum time the algorithm will take as the input size increases.
- **Use case:** Big O is typically used to express the worst-case performance of an algorithm, especially when you want to ensure the algorithm will not exceed a certain time limit.
- **Example:**
    o For a linear search in an unsorted array, the time complexity is **O(n)** because, in the worst case, you have to check each element once.

2. Big Ω Notation (Ω) – Best-Case Time Complexity

- **Definition:** Big Ω notation describes the **lower bound** of an algorithm's running time. It represents the best-case scenario, i.e., the minimum time the algorithm will take.

43

- **Use case:** Big Ω is useful to express the best-case performance when the input is optimal (e.g., when the data is already sorted).
- **Example:**
  - For binary search in a sorted array, the best case is when the target element is found in the middle of the array, which takes **Ω(1)** time.

3. Big Θ Notation (Θ) – Tight Bound

- **Definition:** Big Θ notation provides a **tight bound** on the running time of an algorithm, meaning it describes both the upper and lower bounds. It's used to express the **exact asymptotic behavior** of an algorithm.
- **Use case:** Big Θ is helpful when you want to express the average-case or typical behavior of an algorithm, as it gives both the worst-case and best-case time complexities.
- **Example:**
  - For Merge Sort, the time complexity is **Θ(n log n)** because its worst-case and best-case performance are both the same, regardless of the input.

Summary of Notations:

Notation	Description	Use Case
Big (O)	**O** Upper bound (worst-case)	Worst-case scenario, maximum time complexity
Big (Ω)	**Ω** Lower bound (best-case)	Best-case scenario, minimum time complexity
Big (Θ)	**Θ** Tight bound (exact asymptotic behavior)	Average-case or exact bound for time complexity

Real-World Examples of Complexity Analysis in Choosing Data Structures

Let's look at a few real-world scenarios to understand how **time complexity** and **space complexity** influence the choice of data structures:

1. Web Caching with Hash Tables:

- In web applications, **caching** frequently accessed data (like user profiles) can significantly improve performance.

45

- **Hash tables** are often used for this task because they provide **O(1)** average-time complexity for storing and retrieving data.
- The trade-off is that hash tables require additional **space** to store the hash keys and their corresponding values, which may not be suitable for small memory-constrained environments.

2. Task Scheduling with Priority Queues:

- A **priority queue** can be used in scheduling systems, where tasks must be processed in order of priority.
- A **binary heap** is a popular implementation, where the **insert** and **remove** operations have **O(log n)** time complexity.
- **Space complexity** is **O(n)**, where **n** is the number of tasks, which is reasonable for most scheduling systems, but scaling may require optimized memory usage.

3. Searching in a Large Dataset with Binary Search Trees:

- **Binary Search Trees (BSTs)** provide an efficient way to search, insert, and delete elements with **O(log n)** time complexity, assuming the tree is balanced.
- **AVL trees** or **Red-Black trees** are examples of self-balancing BSTs that ensure logarithmic height for optimal performance.

- However, while these trees provide fast operations, they require **O(n)** space, which is necessary to store the nodes and their pointers.

4. Range Queries with Segment Trees:

- If you need to perform range queries on a dataset (e.g., find the minimum or maximum in a given range), **segment trees** are an excellent choice.
- **Time complexity** for both query and update operations in a segment tree is **O(log n)**, making it ideal for dynamic datasets where the data can change over time.
- **Space complexity** is **O(n)**, where **n** is the size of the input data.

Conclusion

Understanding **Big O**, **Big Ω**, and **Big Θ** notations is essential for analyzing the efficiency of algorithms and data structures. As we've seen in the examples, choosing the right data structure involves balancing **time complexity** and **space complexity** to meet the requirements of the problem at hand. In real-world applications, performance considerations often dictate the choice of algorithms and data structures.

In the next chapter, we will dive into **self-balancing binary search trees**, starting with **AVL trees**, and explore how these structures efficiently manage ordered data with optimal time complexity. Let's continue this journey of mastering advanced data structures!

CHAPTER 4

SELF-BALANCING BINARY
SEARCH TREES (AVL TREES)

In the world of data structures, the need for efficient searching, insertion, and deletion operations is paramount. While **binary search trees (BSTs)** offer a basic solution for ordered data storage, they can suffer from **inefficiency** when the tree becomes unbalanced. An unbalanced BST can degrade into a **linked list**, where operations that would normally take **O(log n)** time, such as searching or insertion, could end up taking **O(n)** time in the worst case.

This is where **self-balancing binary search trees**, specifically **AVL trees**, come into play. An **AVL tree** ensures that the tree remains balanced after every insertion and deletion, keeping the time complexities for searching, insertion, and deletion consistently at **O(log n)**.

In this chapter, we will:

- Introduce **AVL trees** and the **concept of balancing**.
- Explain how **rotations** (left and right) are used to maintain balance in AVL trees.

- Provide **practical examples** of how AVL trees are used in real-world applications, such as databases.

Introduction to AVL Trees and the Concept of Balancing

An **AVL tree** is a type of **binary search tree (BST)** that automatically maintains its balance through strict balancing criteria. Named after its inventors **Adelson-Velsky** and **Landis**, AVL trees are one of the earliest and most well-known forms of **self-balancing** binary search trees.

What Makes an AVL Tree Different?

- **Binary Search Tree (BST) Property:** Like any BST, an AVL tree maintains the order property where:
    - All nodes in the left subtree of a node contain values **less than** the node's value.
    - All nodes in the right subtree contain values **greater than** the node's value.
- **Balance Factor:** An AVL tree maintains an additional property to ensure balance. The **balance factor** of any node is calculated as the difference between the heights of its left and right subtrees. Specifically:

- o **Balance Factor = Height of Left Subtree - Height of Right Subtree**

For the tree to remain balanced, the balance factor for each node must be between **-1** and **1**. If the balance factor goes beyond this range, the tree becomes unbalanced, and a rotation is needed to restore balance.

Why Balance Matters:

- An unbalanced tree can degenerate into a **linear structure**, where the tree behaves like a linked list. In such cases, the search, insertion, and deletion operations would take **O(n)** time, which is inefficient.
- By maintaining balance, an AVL tree ensures that the height of the tree is always kept to a **logarithmic** value (**O(log n)**), ensuring efficient operations.

How Rotations (Left and Right) Work to Maintain Balance

When a node is inserted or deleted from an AVL tree, it may cause the balance factor of one or more nodes to exceed the allowed range of -1, 0, or 1. To restore balance, we perform **rotations**. A rotation is a local operation that restructures the tree in a way that maintains the binary search tree property while improving balance.

Types of Rotations:

1. **Right Rotation (Single Rotation):** Right rotation is used when the left subtree of a node becomes too tall (i.e., the balance factor is 2).

   o **Procedure:**
      - Perform a right rotation around the unbalanced node.
      - The left child of the unbalanced node becomes the new root of the subtree, and the original root becomes its right child.

   o **Example:** Consider the following tree, where node X has become unbalanced due to its left subtree:

   markdown

```
    X
   /
  Y
 /
Z
```

   A right rotation around X results in:

52

```
nginx
```

```
    Y
   / \
  Z   X
```

2. **Left Rotation (Single Rotation):** Left rotation is used when the right subtree of a node becomes too tall (i.e., the balance factor is -2).

   o **Procedure:**
   - Perform a left rotation around the unbalanced node.
   - The right child of the unbalanced node becomes the new root of the subtree, and the original root becomes its left child.

   o **Example:** Consider the following tree, where node X has become unbalanced due to its right subtree:

```
markdown
```

```
  X
   \
    Y
     \
      Z
```

A left rotation around X results in:

```markdown

      Y
     / \
    X   Z
```

3. **Left-Right Rotation (Double Rotation):** This occurs when a node has a left-heavy subtree, and the left child itself has a right-heavy subtree. In this case, a **left rotation** is first performed on the left child, followed by a **right rotation** on the unbalanced node.

   o   **Example:** Before the rotation:

   ```markdown

           X
          /
         Y
          \
           Z
   ```

   After performing a left rotation on X followed by a right rotation on X, we get:

   ```nginx

         Z
        / \
       Y   X
   ```

4. **Right-Left Rotation (Double Rotation):** This is the opposite of the left-right rotation. It occurs when a node has a right-heavy subtree, and the right child itself has a left-heavy subtree. A **right rotation** is performed on the right child first, followed by a **left rotation** on the unbalanced node.

   o **Example:** Before the rotation:

   markdown

```
    X
     \
      Y
     /
    Z
```

   After performing a right rotation on Y followed by a left rotation on X, we get:

   nginx

```
    Z
   / \
  X   Y
```

Practical Examples of AVL Trees in Real Applications

AVL trees are widely used in systems that require efficient data retrieval, insertion, and deletion, where maintaining balance ensures optimal performance. Here are some practical examples of how AVL trees are used in real-world applications:

1. Database Indexing:

- In database management systems (DBMS), **AVL trees** are often used for indexing data. Since databases store large amounts of data, ensuring fast search and update operations is critical. AVL trees allow for efficient searching, insertion, and deletion while maintaining the **sorted order** of the data.
- **Example:** A **database index** implemented using an AVL tree can efficiently search for records, update them, or delete them with logarithmic time complexity, ensuring fast access to large datasets.

2. Memory Management:

- AVL trees are sometimes used in **memory management** systems to track available and allocated memory blocks. By maintaining balance, the system can efficiently allocate and deallocate memory, ensuring that memory management operations are fast and scalable.
- **Example:** An AVL tree can store memory blocks in such a way that when new blocks are allocated, the system can

quickly find the most suitable block, and when blocks are freed, they can be efficiently reinserted into the tree.

3. File Systems:

- Some **file systems** use AVL trees to manage the metadata of files and directories. In these systems, AVL trees provide fast access to file and directory names, ensuring that file-related operations (e.g., searching, adding, or deleting files) are handled efficiently.
- **Example:** File systems like **ZFS** or **ext4** use tree-based structures to maintain directory structures and efficiently access files within large storage systems.

4. Memory Allocation in Operating Systems:

- In operating systems, **AVL trees** are used in **dynamic memory allocation** systems. The operating system needs to allocate and free memory blocks efficiently, especially in real-time environments. AVL trees ensure that this process remains fast, even as the memory usage grows.
- **Example:** The **buddy memory allocation** algorithm in some operating systems uses AVL trees to manage free memory blocks efficiently, ensuring low-latency memory allocation and deallocation.

5. Autocomplete Systems:

- In applications like search engines or text editors, **AVL trees** can be used in **autocomplete systems** to store a dictionary of words and provide quick search results based on user input. Since the tree is always balanced, it ensures fast retrieval of the most relevant suggestions.

- **Example:** When a user types the first few letters of a word, the system can quickly search through the tree for possible completions, providing real-time suggestions.

Conclusion

In this chapter, we have explored the foundational concepts of **AVL trees**, including their balance factor, the importance of maintaining balance in a binary search tree, and the techniques of **rotations** used to achieve this balance. We also discussed several practical applications of AVL trees in real-world systems, such as **databases, file systems**, and **memory management**.

By ensuring that the tree remains balanced at all times, AVL trees provide efficient **O(log n)** time complexity for searching, insertion, and deletion operations, making them an invaluable tool for applications that require high performance with large datasets.

In the next chapter, we will delve deeper into **Red-Black Trees**, which are another type of self-balancing binary search tree, and compare them to AVL trees to understand the trade-offs between the two structures.

CHAPTER 5

RED-BLACK TREES: BALANCED BINARY SEARCH TREES

In this chapter, we will explore **Red-Black Trees** (RBTs), a self-balancing binary search tree that offers an alternative to **AVL trees** for maintaining balanced data. Both AVL trees and Red-Black Trees are designed to maintain the **logarithmic height** of a tree, ensuring efficient searching, insertion, and deletion. However, they achieve balance through different mechanisms, and understanding these differences can help in choosing the right tree structure for specific applications.

We will discuss:

- The **differences between AVL trees and Red-Black trees**, including their balancing strategies and performance characteristics.
- The **rotations and color properties** of Red-Black trees that help maintain balance during insertions and deletions.
- The **use cases** for Red-Black Trees, particularly in scenarios where maintaining ordered data efficiently is crucial (e.g., Java's `TreeMap`).

Differences Between AVL Trees and Red-Black Trees

Both **AVL trees** and **Red-Black trees** are types of **self-balancing binary search trees**, but they differ in terms of **balance criteria**, **rotation frequency**, and **performance**. Let's compare the two to understand the trade-offs.

1. Balance Factor and Height of the Tree:

- **AVL Trees:**
    - An AVL tree maintains a stricter balance criterion. For each node, the difference between the heights of the left and right subtrees (the **balance factor**) can only be -1, 0, or +1.
    - This means the AVL tree is **more rigidly balanced** and the height of the tree is always kept close to **log n**.
    - As a result, AVL trees tend to be **more balanced** than Red-Black trees, but maintaining this balance requires more frequent rotations during insertion and deletion.
- **Red-Black Trees:**
    - In contrast, Red-Black trees have a **less strict balancing criterion**. A Red-Black tree uses a set

61

of properties related to the colors of nodes (red and black) to ensure balance, but the **balance factor** can vary more freely than in AVL trees.

- o The height of a Red-Black tree is bounded by **2 * log n** (rather than log n), meaning Red-Black trees can tolerate **slightly more imbalance**.
- o Because of the **less strict balancing** criteria, Red-Black trees perform fewer rotations on average than AVL trees, making them more efficient for certain types of applications.

2. Rotations and Balancing Cost:

- **AVL Trees:**
  - o In AVL trees, balancing occurs through rotations after each insertion or deletion, and the number of rotations required is proportional to the height of the tree (log n).
  - o Because AVL trees enforce stricter balance, they require more frequent rotations compared to Red-Black trees, particularly when insertions and deletions occur in sequences that would cause imbalance.
- **Red-Black Trees:**
  - o Red-Black trees perform rotations as well, but due to the less strict balance criteria, **rotations happen less frequently**.

- o Red-Black trees typically require fewer rotations, especially during insertion and deletion, which leads to better **amortized performance** in dynamic datasets.

3. Tree Height and Performance:

- **AVL Trees:**
  - o The height of an AVL tree is tightly constrained to **log n** due to the strict balance condition.
  - o As a result, operations like **search**, **insert**, and **delete** can be guaranteed to be very efficient, with **O(log n)** time complexity.
  - o However, the overhead of maintaining the balance can slow down operations when there are frequent insertions and deletions.
- **Red-Black Trees:**
  - o The height of a Red-Black tree is at most **2 * log n**, which means Red-Black trees can tolerate a bit more imbalance.
  - o While search, insert, and delete operations still run in **O(log n)** time on average, they can sometimes be slower than AVL trees due to the slightly higher height of the tree.
  - o Despite this, Red-Black trees are **faster on average** when it comes to insertion and deletion due to fewer rotations.

Rotations and Color Properties of Red-Black Trees

1. Color Properties:

The fundamental concept behind Red-Black trees is the **coloring** of nodes. Each node in a Red-Black tree is either **red** or **black**. The tree must satisfy the following five properties:

1. **Root Property:** The root is always black.
2. **Leaf Property:** Every leaf (NIL node) is black.
3. **Red Property:** If a red node has children, then both its children must be black (no two red nodes can be adjacent).
4. **Black Property:** Every path from a node to its descendants' leaves must contain the same number of black nodes.
5. **Balance Property:** The number of black nodes from the root to any leaf is always the same, ensuring that no path is more than twice as long as any other.

These properties help ensure that the tree remains balanced while still allowing for efficient insertion and deletion operations.

2. Rotations in Red-Black Trees:

Just like in AVL trees, Red-Black trees use rotations to restore balance when the tree becomes unbalanced. There are two primary types of rotations used in Red-Black trees:

- **Left Rotation:** A left rotation is used when the right child of a node is too tall (i.e., causes imbalance due to a violation of the red property).

    o **Example:** Before left rotation:

    markdown

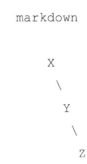

    After left rotation:

    markdown

```
        Y
       / \
      X   Z
```

- **Right Rotation:** A right rotation is used when the left child of a node is too tall.

65

o **Example:** Before right rotation:

markdown

```
    X
   /
  Y
 /
Z
```

After right rotation:

markdown

```
    Y
   / \
  Z   X
```

3. Double Rotations:

Just like in AVL trees, Red-Black trees also require **double rotations** (left-right or right-left) when the imbalance occurs at a **diagonal** position in the tree.

- **Left-Right Rotation:** This is required when a left child's right subtree becomes taller.
- **Right-Left Rotation:** This is required when a right child's left subtree becomes taller.

Use Cases for Red-Black Trees in Maintaining Ordered Data

Red-Black trees are used in applications where the key requirement is to maintain **ordered data** with efficient insertions, deletions, and lookups. Here are some practical examples:

1. Java's TreeMap *and* TreeSet:

- Java's **TreeMap** and **TreeSet** are built using Red-Black trees. These collections maintain sorted data, and all operations (search, insertion, deletion) are guaranteed to run in **O(log n)** time, thanks to the Red-Black tree structure.
- **Use Case:** A TreeMap is useful when you need a key-value pair collection with fast access to ordered data, such as in applications that require **sorted data**, **range queries**, or **frequency count**.

2. Database Indexing:

- Many database management systems (DBMS) use **Red-Black trees** or similar self-balancing binary search trees to implement **indexes**. These indexes allow for fast searching, inserting, and deleting records based on key values.

- **Use Case:** Red-Black trees can be used for **indexing large datasets**, allowing for fast **range queries**, **insertions**, and **deletions**.

3. Memory Allocation and Scheduling:

- **Red-Black trees** are also used in some **memory allocators** to manage free memory blocks. The tree maintains a sorted list of memory blocks and allows the allocator to quickly find available blocks or merge adjacent free blocks.
- **Use Case:** Operating systems can use Red-Black trees for managing free memory segments and performing **efficient memory allocation**.

4. File System Implementations:

- Red-Black trees are sometimes used in **file systems** to maintain directories, as they allow efficient searching and ordering of files based on their names or other metadata.
- **Use Case:** A Red-Black tree structure can help maintain **sorted directories** in a file system, allowing for quick **search** and **update** operations.

5. Real-Time Systems:

- In **real-time systems** where tasks need to be scheduled in order of priority or deadlines, Red-Black trees can be used to maintain an ordered list of tasks or events.
- **Use Case: Task scheduling** algorithms in real-time operating systems (RTOS) use Red-Black trees to keep tasks ordered by priority and allow for efficient updates when tasks are added or removed.

Conclusion

In this chapter, we explored **Red-Black trees**, which are another form of **self-balancing binary search trees**. We compared them to **AVL trees** to highlight the trade-offs between balance strictness, rotation frequency, and performance. We also discussed the **rotations and color properties** that maintain balance in Red-Black trees, and how they provide efficient solutions for ordered data storage in real-world applications like **Java's TreeMap**, **databases**, and **file systems**.

Red-Black trees strike a balance between maintaining an ordered structure and minimizing the cost of balancing during insertions and deletions. As a result, they are an excellent choice when performance and scalability are important in dynamic environments.

In the next chapter, we will dive into another critical data structure—**B-trees**—and see how they are used in large-scale systems, particularly for **disk-based storage** and **indexing** in databases.

CHAPTER 6

B-TREES: BALANCED SEARCH TREES FOR DISK STORAGE

When working with large datasets that need to be efficiently stored and accessed, especially in situations where data cannot fit entirely into memory, **B-trees** provide a powerful solution. B-trees are a type of **balanced search tree** optimized for systems that read and write large blocks of data, such as **file systems** and **databases**. Unlike traditional binary search trees, B-trees are designed to minimize the number of disk accesses required to search, insert, and delete data.

In this chapter, we will:

- Explore **B-trees** and their use in **file systems** and **databases**.
- Discuss how **B-trees differ from binary search trees** (BSTs) and **AVL trees**, and the advantages they offer for disk-based storage.
- Provide a **real-world example** of how databases like **MySQL** use B-trees for **indexing** to ensure efficient data retrieval.

B-Trees and Their Use in File Systems and Databases

A **B-tree** is a self-balancing search tree data structure that maintains sorted data and allows for efficient insertion, deletion, and search operations. B-trees are particularly effective in systems that manage large datasets, such as **databases** and **file systems**, because they are optimized for systems that rely on disk storage.

Key Properties of B-Trees:

1. **Balanced Structure:**
    - o A B-tree is **balanced**, meaning all leaf nodes are at the same depth. This ensures that the tree maintains **logarithmic height** relative to the number of elements, minimizing the number of disk accesses required for search operations.

2. **Nodes Contain Multiple Keys:**
    - o Unlike binary search trees (BSTs), where each node holds only one key, a B-tree node can hold **multiple keys**. This reduces the number of levels in the tree, which is especially important for disk storage, where each node corresponds to a block of data read or written to disk.

3. **Efficient Disk Access:**

o B-trees are designed to minimize the number of disk accesses required. Disk access is slow compared to **memory access**, so B-trees are structured to reduce the number of **disk reads**. Nodes in a B-tree are large enough to hold many keys, ensuring that a search operation requires fewer reads from the disk.

4. **High Fanout:**

   o The **fanout** of a B-tree (the number of children each node can have) is **high**. This high fanout helps to keep the height of the tree small, reducing the number of disk accesses required to traverse the tree.

Operations on B-Trees:

- **Search:** Searching for a key in a B-tree is done by traversing the tree from the root to the leaf nodes. Each node contains a range of keys, and a search only needs to check the appropriate key range within each node, making search operations **O(log n)**.
- **Insertion and Deletion:** Insertion and deletion in B-trees require balancing the tree by splitting or merging nodes to ensure that the tree remains balanced. Both operations can be completed in **O(log n)** time, and because nodes can hold multiple keys, these operations are optimized for **bulk insertions** or deletions.

How B-Trees Differ from Binary Search Trees and AVL Trees

While **binary search trees (BSTs)** and **AVL trees** are commonly used in memory, B-trees are optimized for disk-based storage systems. The fundamental differences between these trees revolve around how data is stored, the balancing criteria, and how the trees handle disk accesses.

1. Structure and Node Capacity:

- **Binary Search Trees (BSTs):**
  - In a **BST**, each node contains a single key and has two children (left and right). For a balanced BST, the time complexity for search, insertion, and deletion is **O(log n)**.
  - However, in a typical **memory-based BST**, there is no need to worry about the number of keys stored in each node. As a result, the height of a BST can grow with an increasing number of nodes, especially when the tree is unbalanced.
- **AVL Trees:**
  - **AVL trees** are a specific type of **self-balancing binary search tree**. They enforce a strict balance

factor condition (the difference in height between left and right subtrees must be -1, 0, or +1).

- o While AVL trees offer logarithmic time complexity for searching, inserting, and deleting, the cost of balancing operations (rotations) can be higher due to the strict balancing requirements, which makes AVL trees less efficient for disk-based storage.

- **B-Trees:**
  - o A **B-tree** node can store multiple keys, significantly reducing the **height** of the tree. The tree is designed so that each node contains multiple children, which minimizes the number of levels in the tree and reduces disk access time.
  - o **Disk Access Efficiency:** B-trees are optimized for environments where accessing memory (or disk blocks) is costly. By having larger nodes, B-trees ensure fewer reads and writes, which is crucial for performance in **disk-based storage systems**.
  - o B-trees also support efficient **range queries** since the nodes are stored in sorted order.

2. Balance Criteria:

- **BSTs and AVL Trees:**

- o **Binary search trees** (BSTs) and **AVL trees** focus on ensuring that nodes are placed in a sorted order, but do not optimize for **minimizing disk reads**.
- o **AVL trees** are **more strictly balanced** than BSTs, but they still require more frequent rotations compared to B-trees, especially during insertions and deletions, which can be less efficient in systems dealing with large datasets stored on disk.

- **B-Trees:**
  - o **B-trees** maintain a balance through a different mechanism. They allow each node to store multiple keys and children, and instead of enforcing strict balance between left and right subtrees, they focus on ensuring that the tree height remains **logarithmic** relative to the number of entries.
  - o B-trees also **minimize disk reads** by ensuring that each node can hold a large number of keys (depending on the block size of the storage medium). This high **fanout** (the number of children per node) helps keep the tree **shallow**, which is crucial for disk-based storage where each disk read operation can be expensive.

Real-World Example: How Databases Like MySQL Use B-Trees for Indexing

B-trees are commonly used in **database management systems (DBMS)** to implement **indexing** for fast data retrieval. **MySQL,** one of the most widely used relational database systems, uses **B-trees** (specifically **B+ trees**, which are a variant of B-trees) for indexing.

1. B-Tree Indexing in MySQL:

When a database query is executed, the DBMS needs to retrieve records from a table based on certain key values. Without an index, the database would have to perform a **full table scan**, examining each row to find matches. This would be highly inefficient, especially with large datasets.

- **B+ Tree Index:** In MySQL, **B+ trees** are used to implement **primary and secondary indexes**. A **primary index** is typically created on the **primary key** of the table, while **secondary indexes** are created on other frequently queried columns.
- **How B+ Trees Work:**
    o **B+ trees** are similar to B-trees but with a key difference: **only the leaf nodes** of a B+ tree contain the actual data pointers (or references to

77

the data rows), while the internal nodes store keys for navigation.

- o The **leaf nodes** in a B+ tree are linked together in a **linked list** to facilitate efficient range queries. This means that when querying for a range of values (e.g., finding all rows with values between 100 and 500), the DBMS can quickly traverse the leaf nodes without needing to perform multiple searches.

2. Advantages of B-Tree Indexing in Databases:

- **Efficient Search:** B-trees allow for efficient **searching** of records in **logarithmic time**.
- **Range Queries:** B-trees support efficient **range queries** because the leaf nodes are linked together, allowing for quick access to all records within a specific range.
- **Dynamic Updates:** B-trees handle **insertion** and **deletion** of records efficiently by performing a limited number of rotations and maintaining the balance of the tree.
- **Disk Access Optimization:** Because nodes in a B-tree can store multiple keys, the number of disk accesses required for each operation is minimized. This is critical for performance in large-scale systems where disk reads are costly.

Example Query:

Consider a table of employees with an index on the `employee_id` column. When querying for an employee by `employee_id`, MySQL uses the B-tree index to quickly navigate through the tree and retrieve the corresponding record in **O(log n)** time.

- **SQL Query:** `SELECT * FROM employees WHERE employee_id = 12345;`
- **Index Search:** The index search starts at the root of the B-tree and navigates through the internal nodes to reach the leaf node, where the employee record is found.
- **Result:** The corresponding record is retrieved efficiently without a full table scan.

Conclusion

In this chapter, we have explored **B-trees**, a fundamental data structure used in **file systems** and **databases** for efficient disk storage and retrieval of ordered data. By allowing nodes to store multiple keys, B-trees minimize disk accesses, ensuring **logarithmic time complexity** for operations like search, insertion, and deletion.

We also discussed how B-trees differ from other balanced trees like **AVL trees** and **binary search trees** in terms of their

79

structure, balance criteria, and performance characteristics. Finally, we saw a real-world example of how databases like **MySQL** leverage **B+ trees** for indexing, demonstrating their practical application in improving the efficiency of data retrieval.

In the next chapter, we will delve into **Segment Trees**, a data structure designed for efficient **range queries** and updates, often used in applications like **computational geometry** and **real-time systems**.

CHAPTER 7

SPLAY TREES: SELF-ADJUSTING BINARY SEARCH TREES

In the realm of self-balancing binary search trees, **splay trees** offer a unique approach to maintaining balance. Unlike traditional self-balancing trees like AVL or Red-Black trees, **splay trees** do not strictly maintain a balanced structure at all times. Instead, they rely on a dynamic, **self-adjusting** mechanism that moves recently accessed elements closer to the root, ensuring that frequently accessed elements can be found quickly in the future.

In this chapter, we will:

- Explore the **concept of splay trees** and how they adjust themselves dynamically.
- Discuss the idea of **amortized time complexity**, which is crucial for understanding the performance of splay trees.
- Examine real-world applications of **splay trees**, particularly in **caching** and **data compression**, to see how they provide practical solutions to performance challenges.

Understanding Splay Trees and Their Self-Adjusting Mechanism

A **splay tree** is a **self-adjusting binary search tree**. The key characteristic of a splay tree is that it performs an operation called a **splay** whenever a node is accessed (whether for searching, insertion, or deletion). The **splay operation** moves the accessed node to the root of the tree by performing a series of tree rotations.

Splay Operation:

The **splay operation** involves a sequence of rotations to move a node to the root. These rotations are **left rotations** and **right rotations** (similar to AVL and Red-Black trees), but the key difference is that the splay operation doesn't always maintain a perfectly balanced tree. Instead, it adapts the tree based on recent access patterns.

- **Basic Steps of Splaying:**
    1. **Zig Rotation:** If the node is the child of the root, perform a single rotation to bring it to the root.
    2. **Zig-Zig Rotation:** If the node and its parent are both on the same side (either both left or both right), perform two rotations in the same direction to bring the node to the root.

3. **Zig-Zag Rotation:** If the node and its parent are on opposite sides (one left and one right), perform a zig-zig rotation followed by a zig rotation.

These rotations are designed to move the accessed node up the tree, with the **most recently accessed nodes** being moved closer to the root, which optimizes future access times for those nodes.

Example:

Consider the following splay tree:

```markdown

        20
       /  \
     10    30
    /  \
   5    15
```

If we access node 15, the splay operation will bring it to the root. This will involve a **zig-zag rotation** since 15 is the right child of 10 (its parent) and the left child of 20 (its grandparent):

1. **Zig-Zag Rotation**: Rotate 15 up to become the root, with 10 and 20 becoming the children of 15.

After the splay operation, the tree will look like this:

markdown

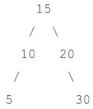

```
    15
   /  \
  10   20
  /     \
 5       30
```

In this new structure, the most recently accessed node (15) is at the root, making future access to this node faster.

The Concept of Amortized Time Complexity

One of the main benefits of splay trees is their **amortized time complexity**. Amortized analysis is used to understand the average time required per operation over a sequence of operations, rather than looking at the worst-case time for a single operation.

Why Amortized Time Complexity?

- While individual splay operations may take **O(n)** time in the worst case (when the tree becomes degenerate like a linked list), the **amortized** time complexity for a sequence of operations is **O(log n)**.
- This means that over a sequence of operations, the average cost per operation is logarithmic, even though

some individual operations may take longer. The key idea behind this is that **the cost of an expensive operation is "spread out" over multiple cheaper operations**.

How Amortized Complexity Works:

- Splay trees take advantage of the **recent access patterns** by bringing frequently accessed nodes closer to the root. As a result, over a sequence of operations, the cost of accessing nodes becomes more balanced.
- **Potential Function Method:** The amortized cost of an operation is often calculated using a potential function. The idea is that the cost of each operation is based on the **change in the potential** of the tree after the operation, plus the actual cost of the operation.

In the case of a splay tree, the **amortized time complexity** for search, insertion, and deletion operations is **O(log n)**, because the number of rotations required for each operation grows logarithmically in the average case.

Real-World Applications of Splay Trees

While splay trees are not as widely used as other balanced binary search trees (like AVL trees or Red-Black trees), they have several **real-world applications** where their self-adjusting nature provides performance benefits, particularly in scenarios where **access patterns exhibit locality** or **frequent access to certain elements** is expected.

1. Caching Systems:

Splay trees are particularly useful in **caching systems**, where frequently accessed items need to be retrieved quickly. In a cache, data that is accessed frequently is often kept closer to the root to make future access faster. This behavior aligns well with the self-adjusting nature of splay trees.

- **Use Case:** A **web cache** that stores web pages or API responses might use a splay tree to keep the most frequently accessed pages near the root. When a user accesses a page, that page is moved to the root of the splay tree, making subsequent access faster.
- **Example:** Suppose you have a cache for a news website that stores articles. As users access articles, the most popular articles move toward the root, and as traffic patterns change, the tree self-adjusts, ensuring that popular content is always accessible with minimal disk reads.

2. Data Compression:

Splay trees can be used in **data compression** algorithms where it's important to frequently access certain patterns or substrings in a sequence of data. Since splay trees move recently accessed nodes closer to the root, they are ideal for maintaining an efficient representation of **frequently occurring substrings**.

- **Use Case:** In **Lempel-Ziv-Welch (LZW)** compression, which is commonly used in formats like GIF and TIFF, a splay tree can be used to store and dynamically update the dictionary of substrings. As the compressor accesses and adds new substrings to the dictionary, it can adjust the tree structure to ensure fast access to frequently used patterns.
- **Example:** In a text compression algorithm, commonly occurring character sequences or patterns are moved up the tree, ensuring that they are quickly available for encoding or decoding operations.

3. Network Routing Algorithms:

Splay trees can be used in **network routing algorithms** where the network topology is subject to frequent changes. In dynamic networks, routing tables are constantly updated, and the splay tree can adjust to bring the most recently used routes to the root, ensuring efficient future lookups.

- **Use Case:** In **load balancing** and **network traffic management**, splay trees can dynamically adjust routing decisions to favor frequently used or high-priority paths, optimizing the overall performance of the network.

87

- **Example:** A **router** that maintains routing tables could use a splay tree to quickly find and update the best routes. Recently used routes (e.g., paths with higher traffic) will be moved to the root, ensuring that future packets are routed more efficiently.

4. Memory Management:

Splay trees can also be applied in **memory management systems** where blocks of memory are allocated and freed dynamically. As certain blocks are allocated or freed more frequently, the splay tree can adjust itself to make these blocks easier to find.

- **Use Case:** A **memory allocator** could use a splay tree to manage free memory blocks. Frequently allocated memory blocks can be moved toward the root, ensuring faster access when they are needed again.
- **Example:** In real-time systems where **memory fragmentation** is a concern, splay trees can help by ensuring that the most frequently used blocks are accessed quickly, reducing fragmentation and improving performance.

Conclusion

In this chapter, we introduced **splay trees**, a type of self-adjusting binary search tree that moves frequently accessed nodes to the root, optimizing future access. We explored the **amortized time complexity** of splay trees, which allows them to provide **O(log n)** time complexity for search, insertion, and deletion operations over a sequence of operations.

We also discussed real-world applications where splay trees excel, such as in **caching systems**, **data compression**, **network routing**, and **memory management**. While splay trees are not as commonly used as AVL trees or Red-Black trees, they offer a unique advantage in scenarios where **access patterns exhibit locality** or where recent access information can be leveraged for improved future performance.

In the next chapter, we will delve into **segment trees**, a powerful data structure for handling **range queries** and updates in **dynamic datasets**.

CHAPTER 8

HEAPS: PRIORITY QUEUES FOR EFFICIENT DATA HANDLING

A **heap** is a special type of binary tree used to efficiently manage a collection of elements, where the elements can be retrieved in a specific order based on a priority. Heaps are most commonly used to implement **priority queues**, a data structure that allows for fast retrieval of the element with the highest (or lowest) priority.

In this chapter, we will:

- Introduce **binary heaps**, including **min-heaps** and **max-heaps**, and explain their key properties.
- Discuss how heaps enable efficient **priority queue operations**, including insertion, deletion, and retrieval of the highest/lowest priority elements.
- Explore real-world use cases, such as in **Dijkstra's shortest path algorithm** and **Huffman coding**, where heaps play a central role in improving algorithm efficiency.

Introduction to Binary Heaps, Min-Heaps, and Max-Heaps

A **heap** is a **binary tree** that satisfies the **heap property**, where the parent node either has a value smaller than (for min-heaps) or larger than (for max-heaps) its children.

1. Binary Heap:

A binary heap is a **complete binary tree** that maintains the heap property. This means:

- A binary heap is a **binary tree** where each node has at most two children.
- It is **complete**, meaning that every level of the tree is fully filled except possibly the last, which is filled from left to right.

There are two types of binary heaps:

- **Min-Heap**: In a **min-heap**, the value of each node is less than or equal to the values of its children. This ensures that the smallest element is always at the root of the tree.
- **Max-Heap**: In a **max-heap**, the value of each node is greater than or equal to the values of its children, ensuring that the largest element is at the root of the tree.

2. Min-Heap:

- In a **min-heap**, the smallest element is always at the root of the tree, and the values of the child nodes are greater than or equal to the value of their parent node.
- **Property**: For every node n, the value of n is less than or equal to the values of its children.
- **Example**:

markdown

```
        3
       / \
      5   8
     / \
    6   7
```

In this min-heap:

- The root (3) is the smallest element.
- Both children of the root (5 and 8) are greater than 3, and the same property holds for the rest of the tree.

3. Max-Heap:

- In a **max-heap**, the largest element is always at the root of the tree, and the values of the child nodes are less than or equal to the value of their parent node.
- **Property**: For every node n, the value of n is greater than or equal to the values of its children.
- **Example**:

markdown

```
       10
      /  \
     6    7
    /  \
   5    3
```

In this max-heap:

- o The root (10) is the largest element.
- o Both children of the root (6 and 7) are smaller than 10, and the same property holds for the rest of the tree.

How Heaps Enable Efficient Priority Queue Operations

A **priority queue** is a data structure that stores elements in order of priority, where each element has an associated priority value. The key operations in a priority queue are:

- **Insert**: Add an element with a given priority.
- **Extract-Min/Extract-Max**: Remove and return the element with the highest or lowest priority.
- **Peek**: Retrieve the element with the highest or lowest priority without removing it.

A **heap** is used to efficiently implement a priority queue because of its structure, which allows for:

- **Efficient Insertions**: Inserting a new element into a heap is efficient because the heap property ensures that the insertion of a new element only requires a logarithmic amount of work to maintain the heap property.
- **Efficient Deletions**: Extracting the root (which contains the highest or lowest priority element) is also efficient because it only requires a logarithmic number of operations to reorder the tree and maintain the heap property.
- **Efficient Lookup**: The element with the highest (or lowest) priority is always at the root of the heap, making it easy to retrieve the highest or lowest priority element in constant time.

Heap Operations:

- **Insert Operation**: Insert the new element at the **next available** position in the last level (to maintain the completeness of the binary tree). Then, **heapify** (or "bubble up") the element to restore the heap property, which takes **O(log n)** time.
- **Extract Operation**: Remove the root (which is the highest or lowest priority element). Then, move the last element to the root and **heapify down** to restore the heap property, which also takes **O(log n)** time.
- **Peek Operation**: The element at the root is returned in constant time **O(1)**.

Use Cases in Algorithms

Heaps are used in a variety of algorithms where priority-based data management is crucial. Below are two prominent use cases where heaps play a central role:

1. Dijkstra's Shortest Path Algorithm:

Dijkstra's algorithm finds the shortest path from a source node to all other nodes in a graph. The algorithm uses a **greedy approach**, always selecting the node with the smallest tentative distance that hasn't yet been processed.

- **Heap Role**: In Dijkstra's algorithm, a priority queue is used to efficiently select the next node to process. The priority queue stores nodes with their tentative distances as priority values. The heap allows for:
  - Efficient retrieval of the node with the smallest tentative distance (extract-min operation).
  - Efficient updating of distances for adjacent nodes (decrease-key operation).

By using a heap, both the **insert** and **extract-min** operations take **O(log n)** time, which significantly reduces the time complexity of the algorithm compared to a linear search.

- **Time Complexity**: With a heap-based priority queue, Dijkstra's algorithm runs in **O((V + E) log V)**, where **V** is the number of vertices and **E** is the number of edges. Without a heap, the time complexity would be **O(V^2)**.

2. Huffman Coding:

Huffman coding is a lossless data compression algorithm that assigns variable-length codes to input characters, with shorter codes assigned to more frequent characters. Huffman coding is used in formats like **ZIP files** and **MP3s**.

- **Heap Role**: A **min-heap** is used to build the Huffman tree. The heap stores nodes with their frequencies, and the two nodes with the lowest frequencies are repeatedly extracted from the heap, combined into a new node, and inserted back into the heap. This process continues until only one node remains, which becomes the root of the Huffman tree.

- o The heap is essential here because it allows efficient extraction of the two smallest elements, which is the core operation of the algorithm.
- **Time Complexity**: The heap operations for extraction and insertion each take **O(log n)** time. Since each element must be inserted and extracted from the heap, the overall time complexity of building the Huffman tree is **O(n log n)**.

Conclusion

In this chapter, we explored **heaps**, focusing on **min-heaps** and **max-heaps** and their role in implementing **priority queues**. We discussed how heaps enable efficient operations such as insertion, deletion, and retrieval of the highest or lowest priority element, all of which can be performed in **O(log n)** time due to the tree structure and heap property.

We also examined two prominent real-world use cases where heaps are critical:

- **Dijkstra's shortest path algorithm**, where heaps allow for efficient retrieval of the next node to process.
- **Huffman coding**, where heaps are used to build the binary tree for data compression.

By understanding how heaps work and where they can be applied, you can leverage this data structure to improve the performance of algorithms in various domains, from **graph theory** to **data compression**.

In the next chapter, we will explore **Trie data structures**, which are specialized for efficient **prefix-based searching** and are widely used in **autocomplete** and **spell checking** applications.

CHAPTER 9

TRIE DATA STRUCTURES: EFFICIENT PREFIX-BASED SEARCHING

When it comes to searching for words or strings, especially in applications like **autocomplete, spell checking**, and **dictionary lookups**, the need for an efficient search algorithm becomes paramount. **Trie data structures** offer an optimized solution to these problems by enabling **prefix-based searching** with fast retrieval and insertion times.

In this chapter, we will:

- Explore **what a trie is** and how it enables fast search and retrieval operations.
- Discuss **real-world applications** of tries in **autocomplete** systems, **dictionary implementations**, and more.
- Provide an **example of implementing a simple trie** for word lookup and demonstrate its usage in practical scenarios.

What is a Trie and How It Enables Fast Search and Retrieval Operations

A **trie** (pronounced as "try") is a specialized tree-like data structure used to store a dynamic set of strings, where each node in the tree represents a character in the string. Tries are primarily used to enable efficient **prefix-based searching**, making them ideal for applications that involve string searching and matching.

Key Characteristics of a Trie:

- **Nodes Represent Characters:** Each node in the trie represents a **single character** of a string, and the root node represents the empty string. Each path from the root to a leaf node represents a complete string.
- **Prefix Matching:** Tries allow for **efficient prefix matching**. The structure of the trie enables searching for all strings with a given prefix in **O(k)** time, where **k** is the length of the prefix.
- **Fast Search and Insert Operations:** Tries enable fast search, insert, and delete operations with **O(k)** time complexity, where **k** is the length of the word being inserted or searched for. This is much faster than searching through a list of words or even a binary search tree.

Trie Structure:

- **Each node** stores:
    - A character from the string.
    - A flag indicating whether the node corresponds to the end of a valid word (a terminal node).
    - A list or dictionary of child nodes representing subsequent characters.
- **Root:** The root node represents the start of all words in the trie.
- **Leaf Nodes:** Leaf nodes represent valid words in the trie, and each node is typically marked with a flag indicating the completion of a word.

Here's a basic example of a trie storing the words **"bat"**, **"ball"**, **"balloon"**, and **"batman"**:

less

```
        root
       /    \
      b      a
    / \    / \
   a   t  l   t
  /      /  / \
 t      l  l   m
         \  \  |
          o  o  a
```

```
    \      \    |
    n      n   |
```

In this trie:

- The path **root -> b -> a -> t** corresponds to the word "bat".
- The path **root -> b -> a -> l -> l** corresponds to the word "ball".
- The path **root -> b -> a -> l -> l -> o -> o -> n** corresponds to the word "balloon".
- The path **root -> b -> a -> t -> m -> a -> n** corresponds to the word "batman".

Search Operation:

To search for a word in a trie, you start at the root and follow the characters in the word, traversing the tree. If you reach a node that doesn't exist for a character in the word, the word isn't in the trie.

- **Example: Search for "bat"**:
    1. Start at the root.
    2. Go to the **b** child node.
    3. From **b**, go to the **a** child node.
    4. From **a**, go to the **t** child node.
    5. Since **t** is a terminal node, "bat" is found in the trie.

102

Insert Operation:

To insert a word, you follow the same process as searching. If a node for a character doesn't exist, you create a new node for that character. At the end of the word, you mark the node as terminal to indicate that it is a valid word.

- **Example: Insert "batman"**:
    1. Start at the root.
    2. Follow the existing nodes for "b", "a", and "t".
    3. Create new nodes for the characters "m", "a", and "n".
    4. Mark the node for "n" as terminal.

Real-World Applications of Tries

Tries are particularly useful in scenarios where **efficient string matching** or **prefix-based searching** is required. Here are some common real-world applications of tries:

1. Autocomplete Systems:

Tries are widely used in **autocomplete** systems to provide real-time suggestions as users type. When the user types a prefix, the trie allows for a fast lookup of all words that start with that prefix.

- **Example:** As you type "ba" in a search engine or a mobile device's keyboard, the system quickly retrieves suggestions like "bat", "ball", "balloon", and "batman" from the trie.

2. Dictionary Implementations:

Tries are ideal for implementing **dictionaries** that store large sets of words or strings. Since each node represents a character, tries allow for fast **prefix-based searches** and word lookups, making them ideal for applications like spell checkers, language models, and more.

- **Example:** A dictionary application can use a trie to quickly check whether a word exists, suggest corrections, or provide autocomplete suggestions.

3. IP Routing:

In **IP routing**, tries are used to represent **routing tables** where prefixes are matched against addresses. Tries efficiently store and look up IP addresses or subnets, ensuring fast routing decisions.

- **Example:** A router can use a trie to store network prefixes, and when it needs to forward a packet, it can use the trie to quickly find the longest matching prefix for the destination IP address.

4. String Matching Algorithms:

Tries can be used in **string matching algorithms** to quickly find all occurrences of a substring within a large text. This is particularly useful in **text search engines** or **bioinformatics** where matching strings in large datasets is a common task.

- **Example:** A search engine can use a trie to quickly search through an index of web pages for a given keyword or phrase.

5. Data Compression:

Tries are also used in **data compression** algorithms, such as **LZW (Lempel-Ziv-Welch)** compression. In these algorithms, tries help in maintaining and efficiently updating the dictionary of patterns or substrings found in the data.

- **Example:** In **image compression** or **text compression**, tries are used to dynamically build and update the dictionary of frequently occurring substrings for efficient encoding.

Example of Implementing a Simple Trie for Word Lookup

Here's a simple implementation of a **Trie** in Python to demonstrate its basic operations (insertion and lookup):

python

```python
class TrieNode:
    def __init__(self):
        self.children = {}
        self.is_end_of_word = False

class Trie:
    def __init__(self):
        self.root = TrieNode()

    def insert(self, word):
        node = self.root
        for char in word:
            if char not in node.children:
                node.children[char] = TrieNode()
            node = node.children[char]
        node.is_end_of_word = True

    def search(self, word):
        node = self.root
        for char in word:
            if char not in node.children:
                return False
            node = node.children[char]
        return node.is_end_of_word
```

```
# Example usage
trie = Trie()
trie.insert("bat")
trie.insert("ball")
trie.insert("batman")

print(trie.search("bat"))       # True
print(trie.search("ball"))      # True
print(trie.search("balloon"))   # False
print(trie.search("batman"))    # True
```

Explanation:

- **TrieNode class**: Each node represents a character and contains a dictionary of children (subsequent characters) and a boolean flag is_end_of_word to mark the end of a valid word.

- **Trie class**: The insert method adds words to the trie, and the search method checks whether a word exists in the trie.

- **Example Usage**: We insert the words "bat", "ball", and "batman" and then search for these words. The search function returns True if the word exists in the trie and False otherwise.

Conclusion

In this chapter, we have explored **tries**—a powerful data structure for efficient **prefix-based searching** and **string matching**. We learned that tries enable fast operations for inserting, searching, and deleting words, making them ideal for use cases such as **autocomplete**, **dictionary lookups**, **IP routing**, and **data compression**.

We also saw a practical example of implementing a simple trie in Python for word lookup, which can be extended for various applications in real-world systems.

In the next chapter, we will dive into **Segment Trees**, a data structure designed for efficiently handling **range queries** and updates in dynamic datasets, particularly useful in applications like **computational geometry** and **real-time systems**.

CHAPTER 10

SEGMENT TREES: QUERYING AND UPDATING INTERVALS

When working with large datasets where you need to perform **range queries** and **updates** efficiently, traditional data structures like arrays or linked lists may not be suitable due to their time complexity. **Segment trees** provide an elegant solution by enabling both **range queries** and **range updates** to be performed in **logarithmic time**.

In this chapter, we will:

- Introduce **segment trees** and explain their structure and functionality for interval queries.
- Discuss how segment trees can handle **range queries** (like **sum**, **minimum**, and **maximum**) and **range updates** efficiently, all in **O(log n)** time.
- Explore a **real-world example** of segment trees, focusing on **range minimum queries** and their application in **computational geometry**.

Introduction to Segment Trees for Interval Queries

A **segment tree** is a binary tree used for storing intervals or segments. It allows for efficient querying of the segment that contains a given point or overlaps with a given interval, and can also perform updates to intervals in **logarithmic time**.

Basic Structure:

- A segment tree is typically represented as a **binary tree** where each node stores some information about a segment of the data.
- The **leaf nodes** of the segment tree store individual elements of the array or dataset.
- The **internal nodes** store aggregated information (such as sums, minimums, or maximums) about the segments they represent. Each internal node represents a range of values and contains the result of the operation (e.g., sum, minimum) over that range.

Building the Tree:

- The tree is **built recursively**. The leaves represent the individual elements, and each internal node stores the result of applying an operation (like **sum**, **min**, or **max**) to the range of its children.

- The **root** node of the segment tree stores information about the entire range (e.g., the sum or minimum of the entire array).

Example:

Consider the array [1, 3, 5, 7, 9, 11]. To build a segment tree for range sum queries:

1. The **leaf nodes** store individual values of the array:
   [1] [3] [5] [7] [9] [11]
2. The **internal nodes** store the sum of segments:

css

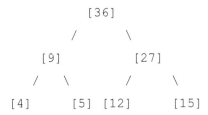

```
            [36]
          /        \
      [9]              [27]
     /   \            /      \
  [4]       [5]  [12]       [15]
```

- o The root node stores the sum of the entire array (36).
- o Internal nodes store the sum of subarrays, for example, the left child of the root stores the sum of [1, 3, 5] which is 9.

111

Range Queries and Updates in Logarithmic Time

The primary benefit of segment trees lies in their ability to perform **range queries** and **range updates** efficiently.

Range Queries:

- A **range query** asks for the result of an operation (sum, minimum, maximum, etc.) over a range of elements in the array.
- In a segment tree, a range query can be answered in **O(log n)** time because each query only requires examining a logarithmic number of nodes in the tree, regardless of the size of the range being queried.

Example: Range Minimum Query (RMQ)

Given an array, we can use a segment tree to answer the query: "What is the minimum value in the range [i, j]?"

1. To query the minimum value between two indices i and j, we traverse the tree, starting from the root.
2. We descend to the relevant segments by checking the nodes that overlap the range [i, j].
3. The segment tree allows us to merge results from the relevant subtrees in **O(log n)** time.

Range Updates:

- **Range updates** involve modifying a range of values in the array. In segment trees, this can be done in **O(log n)** time, thanks to the tree structure and the ability to propagate changes efficiently.
- There are different ways to handle range updates, one of the most common being **lazy propagation**, which allows updates to be applied efficiently without needing to update every single node immediately.

Lazy Propagation for Efficient Range Updates:

- Instead of updating every node for each query, **lazy propagation** allows updates to be delayed (or "lazy") and only propagated to the relevant parts of the tree when necessary.
- This significantly reduces the amount of work during range updates and can make both range queries and updates efficient even with large datasets.

Real-World Example: Range Minimum Queries and Application in Computational Geometry

Segment trees are widely used in a variety of real-world problems, particularly in computational geometry and scenarios involving **intervals** and **ranges**. One of the most common uses of segment trees is to perform **range minimum queries (RMQ)** efficiently.

1. Range Minimum Query (RMQ):

A **range minimum query** asks for the minimum value in a given subarray. This can be useful in many applications, such as finding the shortest path, analyzing data trends, or solving optimization problems.

- **Problem**: Given an array of integers, find the minimum value in the subarray between two indices i and j.
- **Naive Approach**: A naive approach would be to scan through the subarray for every query, which would take **O(n)** time for each query.
- **Segment Tree Approach**: With a segment tree, we can preprocess the array in **O(n)** time and answer each range minimum query in **O(log n)** time.

Example:

Let's consider an array `arr = [1, 3, 2, 7, 9, 11]` and we want to perform range minimum queries on it.

1. Build the segment tree for range minimum queries.

2. For a query asking for the minimum value in the range [2, 5] (i.e., from index 2 to 5), the segment tree will quickly navigate through the tree and find the minimum value, which is 2.

Segment Tree for RMQ:

css

```
              [1, 3, 2, 7, 9, 11]
             /                  \
       [1, 3, 2]             [7, 9, 11]
        /     \               /      \
    [1, 3]   [2]           [7]      [9, 11]
    /    \
  [1]    [3]
```

- For the query [2, 5], the tree will merge the results from the relevant segments (nodes storing the values 2, 7, 9) to quickly return the minimum value, which is 2.

2. Computational Geometry:

In **computational geometry**, segment trees are often used for problems involving **intervals**. A common example is the **interval intersection problem**, where you need to find all intervals that intersect a given query interval.

115

- **Problem**: Given a set of intervals, find all the intervals that overlap with a query interval `[i, j]`.
- **Solution**: By storing intervals in a segment tree, we can perform efficient queries to find all overlapping intervals in **O(log n)** time.

3. Range Updates:

Segment trees with **lazy propagation** are also used to solve problems involving range updates, such as in **range addition** or **range minimum queries with updates**.

- **Problem**: Given an array of integers, increment all values in a given range by a constant value and then query the sum of elements in a range.
- **Solution**: By using a segment tree with lazy propagation, the update can be applied efficiently, and queries can still be answered in **O(log n)** time.

Conclusion

In this chapter, we introduced **segment trees**, a powerful data structure for handling **range queries** and **range updates** efficiently. We saw how segment trees allow for:

- **Range queries** (e.g., range minimum queries) to be answered in **O(log n)** time.

- **Range updates** to be performed efficiently using techniques like **lazy propagation**.

We explored real-world examples such as **range minimum queries** and their application in **computational geometry** and **interval problems**, demonstrating the power of segment trees in efficiently handling range-based operations.

In the next chapter, we will dive into **Fenwick Trees (Binary Indexed Trees)**, another efficient data structure for handling cumulative frequency and prefix sum queries with lower memory requirements compared to segment trees.

CHAPTER 11

FENWICK TREES (BINARY INDEXED TREES)

In the world of data structures, when it comes to handling **prefix sum queries** and **dynamic updates** efficiently, **Fenwick Trees**, also known as **Binary Indexed Trees (BIT)**, offer an elegant and highly efficient solution. Fenwick trees are especially useful when you need to compute cumulative sums over a sequence of data while allowing for frequent updates and queries.

In this chapter, we will:

- Understand the **Fenwick Tree** (or **Binary Indexed Tree**) and how it enables efficient computation of prefix sums.
- Discuss the **difference between Fenwick trees and segment trees**, and when one is preferred over the other.
- Explore practical **applications** of Fenwick trees, such as **calculating cumulative frequencies** and **dynamic data updates**.

Understanding Fenwick Trees for Efficiently Computing Prefix Sums

A **Fenwick Tree** is a binary tree-based data structure that efficiently supports **prefix sum** queries and **point updates**. The primary advantage of Fenwick Trees is their ability to answer range sum queries and perform updates in **O(log n)** time, while using less memory than a segment tree.

How Fenwick Trees Work:

The key concept behind Fenwick Trees is that they represent a cumulative sum structure where each node stores the sum of a specific subset of the array elements. Instead of storing sums for fixed intervals (as in a segment tree), a Fenwick Tree stores partial sums that are defined by the binary representation of the index.

1. **Tree Structure:**
   - A Fenwick Tree is often implemented as an array. The indices in the array are mapped to a **binary tree** structure, but the tree is not explicitly built. Instead, the tree structure is implicitly defined by the indices in the array.
   - Each index in the tree is responsible for the sum of a specific set of elements. These sets overlap, and the indices are chosen based on powers of two.

119

2. **Operations:**

   o **Update Operation:** To update an element at a given index, you modify the corresponding entry in the tree and propagate the change to other relevant indices in **O(log n)** time.

   o **Prefix Sum Query:** To calculate the sum of elements from the start of the array to a given index, you sum the contributions from the relevant tree nodes, which can be done in **O(log n)** time.

Example:

Consider an array `arr = [1, 3, 5, 7, 9, 11]`. To build a Fenwick Tree for prefix sums:

1. Initialize an array `fenwick_tree` of size `n+1` (with all values set to 0).
2. For each index `i`, update the Fenwick Tree by adding the value of `arr[i]` to the tree in the appropriate locations.

After building the tree, the Fenwick Tree might look like this (representing cumulative sums):

```
less
```

```
Fenwick Tree: [0, 1, 4, 5, 12, 9, 20, 11]
```

120

Prefix Sum Query:

To calculate the sum of the first k elements (sum(1, k)), the query proceeds by following the tree structure, accumulating the sum of elements at relevant indices. The time complexity is **O(log n)** due to the logarithmic number of indices involved in the query.

Difference Between Segment Trees and Fenwick Trees

While both **segment trees** and **Fenwick trees** are used to answer range queries and perform updates efficiently, they have some important differences in terms of structure, performance, and use cases.

1. Structure:

- **Segment Tree:**
    - A **segment tree** is typically implemented as a binary tree where each node stores information about a specific segment (or range) of the array.
    - The segment tree is a complete binary tree, and each node can store any type of aggregation (sum, minimum, maximum, etc.) for the range it represents.

121

- **Fenwick Tree (Binary Indexed Tree):**
  - A **Fenwick tree** is typically implemented as a 1D array, with each index implicitly representing a partial sum of the array.
  - Unlike the segment tree, a Fenwick tree doesn't require a full binary tree structure. Instead, it only uses the array and the properties of binary numbers to determine which elements are involved in each query or update.

2. Query and Update Efficiency:

- **Segment Tree:**
  - Segment trees can handle both **range queries** and **range updates** in **O(log n)** time.
  - Segment trees allow for **complex range updates** (e.g., incrementing all elements in a range), which Fenwick trees do not support efficiently.
  - However, the overhead of maintaining a segment tree and storing it as a full binary tree means more memory is used.
- **Fenwick Tree:**
  - Fenwick trees support **point updates** and **prefix sum queries** in **O(log n)** time.
  - They cannot efficiently handle **range updates** directly (without modifications like lazy

propagation), but they are more space-efficient than segment trees.

- o Fenwick trees are generally easier to implement and require less memory because they are represented as a simple array.

3. Memory Usage:

- **Segment Tree:**
  - o A segment tree requires **O(4n)** space, as it stores values for all segments and subsegments.
- **Fenwick Tree:**
  - o A Fenwick tree only requires **O(n)** space, making it more space-efficient, especially for problems that require handling large datasets.

4. Use Cases:

- **Segment Tree:** Best for problems involving **range queries** and **range updates**, especially where multiple types of operations (sum, min, max) are needed.
- **Fenwick Tree:** Best for problems that only require **point updates** and **prefix sum queries**, where space efficiency is important and range updates are not required.

Practical Applications of Fenwick Trees

Fenwick trees are widely used in scenarios where **efficient range sum queries** and **point updates** are required. Some practical applications include:

1. Cumulative Frequency Calculation:

Fenwick trees are frequently used for **cumulative frequency tables** or **frequency counts**, where the goal is to efficiently calculate the frequency of events up to a given index. This is common in applications like **histograms** and **real-time data analysis**.

- **Example:** Suppose you have an array representing the frequency of numbers in a dataset. You can use a Fenwick tree to efficiently calculate the cumulative frequency up to a given index.

2. Dynamic Data Updates:

Fenwick trees allow for efficient **point updates**. This makes them useful in scenarios where data changes frequently, and you need to maintain an aggregate (such as the sum or minimum) over a range of values.

- **Example:** In a stock market application, where the price of a stock changes over time, a Fenwick tree can be used to maintain the running total of stock prices, allowing for quick updates and queries.

3. Range Queries:

Fenwick trees are highly useful in scenarios that require quick calculations of **prefix sums**, **range queries**, or other aggregations (like **sum**, **minimum**, and **maximum**) over a sequence of data.

- **Example:** A **running total** in a financial application or **prefix sum queries** in a dynamic dataset can be efficiently handled using a Fenwick tree.

4. Inversions Count in Arrays:

Fenwick trees can be used to count the number of **inversions** in an array. An inversion is defined as a pair of indices (i, j) such that i < j and arr[i] > arr[j]. A Fenwick tree can help in counting these inversions in **O(n log n)** time.

- **Example:** In a sorting algorithm, Fenwick trees can help calculate the number of inversions in the array, which is crucial for understanding the sortedness of the data.

5. Online Algorithms:

Fenwick trees can be used in **online algorithms** where you receive data incrementally and need to maintain a running calculation. The ability to update and query the tree efficiently is a huge advantage in such scenarios.

Example: Implementing a Fenwick Tree for Prefix Sum

Here's a simple Python implementation of a **Fenwick Tree** for prefix sum queries:

python

```python
class FenwickTree:
    def __init__(self, n):
        self.n = n
        self.tree = [0] * (n + 1)  # Initialize
Fenwick Tree with zero values

    def update(self, index, delta):
        # Update the value at index 'index' by
adding 'delta'
        while index <= self.n:
            self.tree[index] += delta
            index += index & -index  # Move to
the next index in the tree

    def prefix_sum(self, index):
```

126

```
        # Calculate the prefix sum from 1 to
'index'
        result = 0
        while index > 0:
            result += self.tree[index]
            index -= index & -index   # Move to
the parent node
        return result


# Example usage
fenwick = FenwickTree(6)
fenwick.update(1, 1)
fenwick.update(2, 3)
fenwick.update(3, 5)
fenwick.update(4, 7)
fenwick.update(5, 9)
fenwick.update(6, 11)

print(fenwick.prefix_sum(3))   # Output: 9 (1 + 3
+ 5)
print(fenwick.prefix_sum(6))   # Output: 36 (1 +
3 + 5 + 7 + 9 + 11)
```

Explanation:

- The **update** function updates the Fenwick tree by adding `delta` to the value at the specified `index`. It uses the property `index += index & -index` to navigate through the tree.

127

- The `prefix_sum` function calculates the sum of elements from index 1 to `index` by traversing the tree from the given index to the root.

Conclusion

In this chapter, we introduced **Fenwick Trees (Binary Indexed Trees)**, a data structure designed for efficiently handling **prefix sum queries** and **point updates**. We discussed how Fenwick trees work by representing cumulative sums in a binary tree-like structure, and how they can perform both updates and queries in **O(log n)** time.

We also highlighted practical applications, including **cumulative frequency calculations**, **dynamic data updates**, **range queries**, and **inversions counting**. Fenwick trees are particularly useful in scenarios where memory efficiency and fast updates are needed, and they provide a highly efficient alternative to other data structures like segment trees in many cases.

In the next chapter, we will explore **hashing**, a technique used for efficient data retrieval and storage, which is a key component of many advanced algorithms and data structures.

128

CHAPTER 12

DISJOINT SET (UNION-FIND): DYNAMIC CONNECTIVITY

The **disjoint set** data structure, also known as **union-find**, is a powerful tool used to efficiently manage dynamic connectivity problems. It is particularly useful for keeping track of elements that are partitioned into disjoint sets and for determining whether two elements belong to the same set. This data structure supports two main operations: **union** (to combine sets) and **find** (to check if two elements are in the same set).

In this chapter, we will:

- Understand the **basics of disjoint set data structures (union-find)** and their operations.
- Learn about **path compression** and **union by rank**, which optimize the efficiency of the set operations.
- Explore **real-world use cases**, such as **network connectivity** and **Kruskal's algorithm** for finding the minimum spanning tree in a graph.

Basics of Disjoint Set Data Structures (Union-Find)

A **disjoint set** data structure, also called **union-find**, is used to manage a collection of disjoint sets. The primary goal is to keep track of which elements are in which set and to efficiently perform two types of operations:

1. **Find:** Determine which set an element belongs to.
2. **Union:** Merge two sets into one.

Key Operations:

1. **Find Operation:**
   - The `find(x)` operation returns the representative (or **root**) of the set containing x. This representative is used to identify the set to which the element belongs.

2. **Union Operation:**
   - The `union(x, y)` operation merges the sets containing x and y. If the two elements are in different sets, they are joined together.

Initial Representation:

A simple way to represent a disjoint set is to use an array, where each element points to itself initially (indicating that each element is its own set). As we perform union operations, we modify the array to represent merged sets.

For example:

- Initially, each element is its own set:

csharp

```
[0, 1, 2, 3, 4]
```

Here, the element i is in the set {i}.

- After performing a union operation on union(1, 2), the sets of 1 and 2 are merged:

csharp

```
[0, 1, 1, 3, 4]
```

Now, elements 1 and 2 are in the same set, and the representative of this set is 1.

Path Compression and Union by Rank for Efficient Set Operations

While the union and find operations are simple to implement, they can be inefficient if the sets grow too large or are poorly structured. To optimize these operations, we use two key techniques:

1. Path Compression:

Path compression is a technique used to optimize the `find` operation. When we perform a `find(x)` operation, we recursively traverse the tree to find the root. With path compression, we make each node along the path point directly to the root, effectively flattening the tree. This speeds up future `find` operations by reducing the tree height.

- **Without Path Compression:**

  markdown

```
    0
   / \
  1   2
 /
3
```

  If we call `find(3)`, we traverse the path from 3 to 1 and then to 0.

- **With Path Compression:** After performing `find(3)`, we update the parent of 3 to point directly to the root 0:

```markdown
    0
   / \
  1   2
       \
        3
```

2. Union by Rank:

Union by rank is used to optimize the `union` operation. When merging two sets, we attach the smaller tree (in terms of height or rank) to the root of the larger tree. This keeps the tree more balanced, reducing its height and improving the performance of future operations.

- **Without Union by Rank:** If we always attach the second tree to the first tree, the height of the resulting tree can grow linearly, leading to inefficient operations.

```markdown
    0
   /
  1
 /
2
```

133

- **With Union by Rank:** We attach the smaller tree (rank 1) to the larger tree (rank 2), keeping the height smaller.

```markdown
      0
     / \
    1   2
```

Time Complexity:

With both **path compression** and **union by rank**, the amortized time complexity for both `find` and `union` operations becomes nearly constant, specifically **O(α(n))**, where **α(n)** is the **inverse Ackermann function**. This function grows extremely slowly, so for all practical purposes, the time complexity is considered **O(1)**.

Real-World Use Cases

Disjoint set data structures are widely used in a variety of applications that involve **dynamic connectivity** problems, where you need to track the connected components of a set. Some prominent real-world use cases include:

1. Network Connectivity:

Disjoint sets are used to track the connected components of a network. For example, in a **social network**, you might want to check whether two people are in the same group, or in a **communication network**, you might want to check if two devices are connected directly or indirectly.

- **Example:** Given a set of cities and roads between them, a disjoint set data structure can efficiently tell whether two cities are connected by a path or not. As you add new roads, you can update the sets to reflect the new connectivity.

2. Kruskal's Algorithm for Minimum Spanning Tree:

In graph theory, **Kruskal's algorithm** is a greedy algorithm used to find the **minimum spanning tree** (MST) of a connected, weighted graph. The algorithm works by sorting all edges and adding them to the MST one by one, ensuring that no cycles are formed. The disjoint set data structure is used to efficiently check whether adding an edge would form a cycle, by checking if the two vertices of the edge are in the same set.

- **Kruskal's Algorithm Steps**:
    1. Sort all the edges in the graph by weight.
    2. For each edge, check if the two vertices are in the same set using the find operation. If they are not

135

in the same set, add the edge to the MST and combine the sets using the `union` operation.

3. Repeat until all vertices are connected.

- **Time Complexity**: Using a disjoint set with path compression and union by rank, Kruskal's algorithm runs in **O(E log V)** time, where **E** is the number of edges and **V** is the number of vertices.

3. Dynamic Connectivity Problems in Computational Geometry:

In computational geometry, disjoint set data structures are often used to solve dynamic connectivity problems, such as determining if two regions of a map are connected or if two shapes overlap.

- **Example:** Given a set of rectangles on a 2D plane, you can use a disjoint set to determine which rectangles overlap with each other. Each rectangle starts in its own set, and as you process the edges of the rectangles, you union sets when two rectangles overlap.

4. Percolation and Graph Algorithms:

In simulations of percolation (such as for fluid flow through porous materials) or when analyzing large graphs, disjoint sets are used to track clusters or connected components.

- **Example:** In a **percolation model**, you might want to track which sites are connected in a grid. The disjoint set structure efficiently supports dynamic merging of connected sites, allowing you to quickly determine whether there is a path from one point to another.

Example: Implementing Disjoint Set (Union-Find) with Path Compression and Union by Rank

Here's a Python implementation of the **disjoint set** data structure using both **path compression** and **union by rank**:

python

```python
class DisjointSet:
    def __init__(self, n):
        self.parent = list(range(n))    # Parent array
        self.rank = [0] * n             # Rank array for union by rank

    def find(self, x):
        # Path compression
        if self.parent[x] != x:
            self.parent[x] = self.find(self.parent[x])    # Recursively find root and compress path
        return self.parent[x]
```

```python
def union(self, x, y):
    # Find roots of both elements
    rootX = self.find(x)
    rootY = self.find(y)

    # If both have the same root, they are
already in the same set
    if rootX != rootY:
        # Union by rank: attach the smaller
tree to the larger tree
        if      self.rank[rootX]        >
self.rank[rootY]:
            self.parent[rootY] = rootX
        elif        self.rank[rootX]        <
self.rank[rootY]:
            self.parent[rootX] = rootY
        else:
            self.parent[rootY] = rootX
            self.rank[rootX]    +=    1      #
Increment rank if both trees are the same height

# Example usage
ds = DisjointSet(5)
ds.union(0, 1)
ds.union(1, 2)
ds.union(3, 4)

print(ds.find(0))   # Output: 0 (root of 0)
print(ds.find(2))   # Output: 0 (root of 2)
```

```
print(ds.find(3))    # Output: 3 (root of 3)
print(ds.find(4))    # Output: 3 (root of 4)
```

Explanation:

- **find method:** Implements **path compression** to speed up future queries by making all nodes in the path point directly to the root.
- **union method:** Implements **union by rank** to ensure that the smaller tree is always attached to the larger tree, keeping the tree balanced.

Conclusion

In this chapter, we explored **disjoint set data structures (union-find)**, a crucial tool for managing dynamic connectivity problems. We learned how the **find** and **union** operations work, and how **path compression** and **union by rank** optimize these operations. We also discussed the practical applications of disjoint sets in solving problems like **network connectivity**, **Kruskal's algorithm** for minimum spanning trees, and **computational geometry**.

By using disjoint sets, you can efficiently solve dynamic connectivity problems, making them an essential data structure for a wide range of applications in computer science and algorithms.

In the next chapter, we will explore **binary search trees (BSTs)**, a fundamental tree-based structure used to store ordered data efficiently.

CHAPTER 13

HASH TABLES: EFFICIENT DATA STORAGE AND RETRIEVAL

When dealing with large datasets where fast retrieval and updates are essential, **hash tables** provide a powerful solution for **efficient data storage** and **lookup** operations. By leveraging a **hash function**, hash tables enable nearly **constant time complexity** for search, insertion, and deletion operations in the average case, making them ideal for applications like **dictionaries, caches,** and **indexing**.

In this chapter, we will:

- Understand **hash functions**, their role in hash tables, and how they map keys to indices.
- Discuss **collision resolution techniques** and the challenges involved in ensuring efficient table performance.
- Explore **load factors** and how they impact the performance of hash tables.
- Implement a **simple dictionary** or **phone book** using a hash table, demonstrating its practicality and efficiency.

141

Understanding Hash Functions, Collision Resolution Techniques, and Hash Tables

A **hash table** is a data structure that stores data in an array-like format, where each data element (called a **key-value pair**) is mapped to an index using a function called a **hash function**. This allows for efficient data access and modification.

1. Hash Function:

A **hash function** is a function that takes an input (or "key") and maps it to an index in a fixed-size array (called the **hash table**). The goal of the hash function is to distribute keys uniformly across the table, minimizing the chance of **collisions**.

For example, if you have an array of size 10 and a key like 13, the hash function might map 13 to the index $13 \% 10 = 3$. In this case, 3 is the index where the value corresponding to the key 13 will be stored.

2. Collision Resolution Techniques:

A **collision** occurs when two keys hash to the same index in the table. Since each index can only store one key-value pair, collisions must be handled effectively. There are several common methods for resolving collisions:

- **Chaining:** In this approach, each slot of the hash table is a **linked list** (or another data structure). When a collision occurs, the new key-value pair is simply appended to the list at the corresponding index.

  o **Advantages:** Chaining is simple to implement and works well for hash tables with high load factors.

  o **Disadvantages:** Performance can degrade if many elements hash to the same index (i.e., if there are many collisions), leading to longer search times.

- **Open Addressing:** In this method, when a collision occurs, the algorithm searches for the next available slot using a predefined probing sequence (e.g., linear probing, quadratic probing, or double hashing). There are several probing strategies to handle collisions:

  o **Linear Probing:** If a collision occurs at index i, try the next index i + 1, and continue until an empty slot is found.

  o **Quadratic Probing:** Instead of just moving to the next index, quadratic probing moves by i^2, i^2 + 1, i^2 + 4, etc., for each collision.

  o **Double Hashing:** Use a second hash function to determine the next probe position if a collision occurs.

- **Advantages:** Open addressing typically uses less memory than chaining and can be more efficient when there are fewer collisions.
- **Disadvantages:** As the table fills up, performance can degrade significantly, especially for large datasets.

3. Hash Table Structure:

A **hash table** consists of:

- **An array**: The underlying array that stores the key-value pairs.
- **A hash function**: The function used to map keys to indices in the array.
- **A collision resolution strategy**: The method used to handle collisions.

Load Factors and Their Impact on Hash Table Performance

The **load factor** is a measure of how full the hash table is. It is calculated as:

Load Factor=Number of ElementsSize of Hash Table\text{Load Factor} = \frac{\text{Number of Elements}}{\text{Size of Hash Table}}Load Factor=Size of Hash TableNumber of Elements

144

Impact of Load Factor on Performance:

- **High Load Factor:** As the load factor increases, the number of collisions increases. This leads to slower lookup times and more frequent rehashing operations, which can degrade the performance of the hash table.
- **Low Load Factor:** A low load factor means there are fewer collisions, but it can lead to inefficient memory usage because the hash table may have more empty slots than necessary.

To balance these concerns, hash tables typically **resize** (rehash) when the load factor exceeds a certain threshold (e.g., 0.7). When resizing, the hash table is expanded (often doubled in size), and all the elements are rehashed to fit into the new array.

Resizing and Rehashing:

- **Resizing:** When the load factor exceeds a threshold, the table is resized to a larger size, and the elements are rehashed and redistributed in the new table.
- **Rehashing:** Rehashing involves recalculating the indices of all the keys using a new hash function or table size, ensuring that the hash table remains efficient.

Example: Implementing a Simple Dictionary or Phone Book with a Hash Table

Now, let's implement a **simple dictionary** or **phone book** using a hash table. We'll create a hash table to store names as keys and phone numbers as values. We'll use **chaining** to handle collisions.

Step 1: Hash Table Class Definition

We'll implement the hash table with basic operations: **insert**, **lookup**, and **delete**.

python

```python
class HashTable:
    def __init__(self, size=10):
        self.size = size
        self.table = [[] for _ in range(size)]  #
Initialize an empty list for each index

    def hash_function(self, key):
        return hash(key) % self.size   # Basic
hash function that uses Python's built-in hash

    def insert(self, key, value):
        index = self.hash_function(key)
        for i, (k, v) in enumerate(self.table[index]):
            if k == key:
```

```
                self.table[index][i]    =    (key,
value)    # Update the value if the key already
exists
                return
        self.table[index].append((key,    value))
# Add the key-value pair if the key does not exist

    def lookup(self, key):
        index = self.hash_function(key)
        for k, v in self.table[index]:
            if k == key:
                return v    # Return the value
associated with the key
        return None   # Return None if the key is
not found

    def delete(self, key):
        index = self.hash_function(key)
        for      i,       (k,       v)        in
enumerate(self.table[index]):
            if k == key:
                del self.table[index][i]      #
Remove the key-value pair
                return True
        return False   # Return False if the key
is not found
```

147

Step 2: Using the Hash Table for a Phone Book

Now, let's use the hash table to implement a simple phone book where we can store names and phone numbers, look up a phone number by name, and delete an entry.

python

```python
# Create a phone book using the HashTable class
phone_book = HashTable()

# Insert some contacts
phone_book.insert("Alice", "555-1234")
phone_book.insert("Bob", "555-5678")
phone_book.insert("Charlie", "555-8765")

# Look up some contacts
print(phone_book.lookup("Alice"))      # Output:
555-1234
print(phone_book.lookup("Bob"))        # Output:
555-5678
print(phone_book.lookup("Eve"))        # Output:
None (not found)

# Delete a contact
phone_book.delete("Bob")
print(phone_book.lookup("Bob"))        # Output:
None (Bob is deleted)
```

Explanation:

- **hash_function:** This function maps the key (name) to an index in the table using Python's built-in `hash()` function and the table size.
- **insert:** The `insert` method first checks if the key already exists at the calculated index. If it does, it updates the value; otherwise, it adds a new key-value pair.
- **lookup:** The `lookup` method searches for the key in the table and returns the corresponding value.
- **delete:** The `delete` method removes a key-value pair from the table.

Conclusion

In this chapter, we explored **hash tables**—a data structure that provides efficient **data storage** and **retrieval** through the use of **hash functions**. We learned about:

- **Collision resolution techniques**, such as **chaining** and **open addressing**.
- The importance of the **load factor** and how it affects performance, along with the concept of **rehashing**.

- We implemented a **simple dictionary or phone book** using a hash table and demonstrated basic operations like **insert**, **lookup**, and **delete**.

Hash tables are widely used in applications such as **databases**, **caching**, and **symbol tables** in compilers, where fast access to data is essential. In the next chapter, we will delve into **graphs**, a more advanced data structure used to represent networks, relationships, and connections in complex systems.

CHAPTER 14

SKIP LISTS: PROBABILISTIC ALTERNATIVE TO BALANCED TREES

When it comes to efficiently searching, inserting, and deleting data in large datasets, **balanced trees** like **AVL trees** and **Red-Black trees** are commonly used. However, another data structure that provides similar functionality with a different approach is the **skip list**. **Skip lists** offer a probabilistic method of achieving balanced performance for search, insertion, and deletion operations, while being conceptually simpler to implement and understand than traditional balanced trees.

In this chapter, we will:

- Understand **skip lists** and how they enable efficient **search**, **insertion**, and **deletion** operations.
- Compare skip lists to **balanced trees** like **AVL trees** and **Red-Black trees** to highlight their strengths and trade-offs.

- Explore **real-world applications** of skip lists, particularly in **distributed databases**, where they are used for efficient data indexing and retrieval.

Skip Lists and How They Provide Efficient Search, Insertion, and Deletion

A **skip list** is a **probabilistic data structure** that is an alternative to balanced trees, providing an efficient way to store ordered elements while allowing fast search, insertion, and deletion operations. It is essentially a **linked list** that is augmented with **multiple levels** of pointers, enabling faster traversal by "skipping" over many elements.

Skip List Structure:

A skip list consists of multiple layers of linked lists:

1. **Bottom Layer (Level 0):** This is a regular sorted linked list that holds all the elements in the collection.
2. **Upper Layers:** Each higher level is a "shortcut" to multiple elements from the level below. These layers allow us to "skip" over many elements in the bottom layer, thereby improving the search performance.

152

How It Works:

- **Elements in the Skip List:** Each element in the skip list is part of the bottom layer, and as you go up to higher levels, each element at a level has fewer connections. The idea is that the higher levels provide faster access to elements by skipping over intermediate elements.

- **Levels in the Skip List:** The number of levels in the skip list is determined probabilistically. When inserting a new element, a random decision is made about how many levels the element will occupy, which ensures that, on average, the skip list remains balanced. This randomization helps achieve an average time complexity of **O(log n)** for search, insertion, and deletion operations.

Operations in a Skip List:

- **Search Operation:**
  - To search for an element, you start at the topmost level and work your way down. At each level, you traverse the list from left to right, "skipping" over elements to find the right one. Once you reach the bottom level, you perform a final linear search to find the element.
  - This search process is **O(log n)** on average because each level skips over approximately half of the elements at the level below.

153

- **Insertion Operation:**
  - To insert an element, you first search for the appropriate position in the bottom level. After finding the correct position, you randomly decide how many levels the new element should occupy.
  - For each level the element occupies, you adjust the pointers in the relevant linked lists to insert the element at the correct position.
- **Deletion Operation:**
  - To delete an element, you search for it and then remove it from the corresponding levels. If the element exists at multiple levels, you update the pointers at all levels where the element is found.
  - Deletion also occurs in **O(log n)** time on average.

Visual Representation of a Skip List:

Here's an example of a skip list with multiple levels. The bottom level contains all the elements, and higher levels skip over some of them:

```rust
Level 3:          5 ---------> 15 ---------> 40 --
-------> 70
Level 2:    5 ---------> 15 ---------> 40
Level 1: 5 -----> 10 -----> 15 -----> 20 ----->
40 -----> 50
```

154

```
Level 0: 5 -----> 10 -----> 15 -----> 20 ----->
40 -----> 50 -----> 60 -----> 70
```

In this skip list:

- The bottom level (Level 0) holds all the elements.
- Each higher level skips over some of the elements, making it easier to perform a search by jumping over large portions of the list.

How Skip Lists Compare to Balanced Trees (e.g., AVL, Red-Black Trees)

Skip lists provide similar functionality to **balanced trees** such as **AVL trees** and **Red-Black trees**, but they have some distinct advantages and trade-offs.

1. Balanced Trees (AVL Trees and Red-Black Trees):

- **Structure:** Balanced trees are typically implemented as **binary trees**, where each node has two children. These trees ensure that the height of the tree is balanced, which guarantees that operations like search, insertion, and deletion occur in **O(log n)** time.
- **Balancing Mechanism:** Trees like **AVL trees** and **Red-Black trees** maintain balance through specific balancing

rules. For example, AVL trees enforce a strict balance condition on the heights of subtrees, while Red-Black trees maintain balance using color-based rules.

- **Complexity:** Implementing balanced trees requires more complex code and tree rotations during insertion and deletion to maintain balance.

2. Skip Lists:

- **Structure:** A skip list is a **probabilistic** data structure, meaning it doesn't guarantee balance at all times but relies on randomization to ensure that, on average, the height of the list remains logarithmic. The structure is simpler to implement than balanced trees.

- **Insertion and Deletion:** In skip lists, insertion and deletion are probabilistic. Instead of maintaining strict balance through rotations, skip lists adjust the height of each element based on randomization.

- **Performance:** Skip lists offer **O(log n)** time complexity for search, insertion, and deletion, but the actual constant factors may be higher than those for balanced trees due to the overhead of managing multiple levels of linked lists.

Key Differences:

- **Ease of Implementation:** Skip lists are easier to implement than balanced trees like AVL or Red-Black trees because they avoid complex tree rotations and instead rely on probabilistic balancing.

- **Memory Usage:** Skip lists use more memory than balanced trees because each element in the skip list may occupy multiple levels in the list, requiring additional pointers.

- **Performance Guarantees:** Balanced trees guarantee **O(log n)** time complexity for all operations, while skip lists provide average-case **O(log n)** performance but with probabilistic guarantees. In the worst case, operations in a skip list can take **O(n)** time if the levels become unbalanced (although this is rare).

Real-World Application Example: Skip Lists in Distributed Databases

One of the most prominent real-world applications of skip lists is in **distributed databases**, particularly in systems that require **efficient indexing** and **fast data retrieval** across distributed nodes.

1. Distributed Key-Value Stores:

Skip lists are often used in **distributed key-value stores** like **Cassandra** and **Redis** for managing indexes. These databases

157

require efficient access to data in order to quickly retrieve values based on a key or range of keys.

- **Range Queries:** Skip lists provide an efficient way to perform range queries (e.g., retrieving all records between a start and end key) in logarithmic time. This is especially useful in databases where you need to query a range of keys without scanning the entire dataset.

- **Efficient Insertion and Deletion:** As distributed databases grow, the ability to efficiently insert or delete records is crucial. Skip lists allow these operations to be performed efficiently without the need for complex restructuring, as in balanced trees.

2. Example: Cassandra's Use of Skip Lists:

In **Apache Cassandra**, a distributed database, skip lists are used for managing **secondary indexes**. The database relies on skip lists to efficiently store and search large datasets distributed across many nodes.

- **Indexing with Skip Lists:** When a new record is inserted, a **secondary index** (which could be based on the values of a column other than the primary key) is updated using a skip list. This allows for **efficient retrieval** of rows based on non-primary key values.

- **Range Queries:** Cassandra can also perform **range queries** on indexed columns using skip lists, making it much faster than performing a full scan of the data.

Conclusion

In this chapter, we introduced **skip lists**, a probabilistic data structure that provides efficient **search, insertion,** and **deletion** operations, with **O(log n)** time complexity on average. We compared skip lists to **balanced trees** like **AVL trees** and **Red-Black trees**, noting the trade-offs between simplicity, memory usage, and performance.

We also explored the **real-world applications** of skip lists, particularly in **distributed databases** like **Cassandra** and **Redis**, where they are used for efficient **indexing, range queries,** and **dynamic updates**.

Skip lists offer a simple yet powerful alternative to balanced trees in many scenarios where probabilistic balancing is acceptable and efficiency is crucial. In the next chapter, we will dive into **tries**, another important data structure used for efficient **prefix-based searching** and **string matching**.

CHAPTER 15

BLOOM FILTERS: SPACE-EFFICIENT PROBABILISTIC DATA STRUCTURE

In the world of data storage and retrieval, especially when dealing with large datasets, **space efficiency** and **time efficiency** are crucial factors to consider. When it comes to testing whether an element is part of a set, **Bloom filters** provide a **space-efficient, probabilistic** solution that allows for **constant time membership testing** with some trade-offs.

In this chapter, we will:

- Introduce **Bloom filters** and explain how they are used for **set membership testing**.
- Explore the **false positive probability** of Bloom filters and discuss the **trade-off between time and space**.
- Examine **real-world examples** where Bloom filters are applied, such as **web caching** and **spam detection**.

Introduction to Bloom Filters and Their Use in Set Membership Testing

A **Bloom filter** is a **probabilistic** data structure used to test whether an element is a member of a set. Unlike traditional data structures (e.g., arrays, hash tables), Bloom filters do not store the elements themselves. Instead, they use a **bit array** and a set of **hash functions** to represent the set of elements.

Basic Concept:

- The Bloom filter works by applying multiple hash functions to an element and mapping the resulting values to indices in a **bit array**.
- For each element, the corresponding positions in the bit array are set to 1.
- To check whether an element is in the set, the same hash functions are applied to the element. If all the corresponding bits are set to 1, the element **probably** exists in the set. If any of the corresponding bits are 0, the element definitely does **not** exist in the set.

Why Use a Bloom Filter?

- **Space Efficiency:** Bloom filters use significantly less memory compared to other data structures like hash tables or arrays. They can test for membership in large sets without needing to store all the elements.

- **Constant Time Testing:** Bloom filters provide **constant time membership testing** for whether an element is in the set, making them extremely fast for large datasets.

Bloom Filter Operations:

1. **Insert:** To insert an element, you apply multiple hash functions to the element, and for each resulting hash, set the corresponding bit in the array to 1.
2. **Membership Test:** To test if an element is in the set, you apply the same hash functions and check if all the corresponding bits in the bit array are 1. If they are, the element **may** be in the set. If any of the bits are 0, the element is definitely **not** in the set.

False Positive Probability and the Trade-off Between Time and Space

While Bloom filters offer significant space efficiency and fast membership testing, they come with a **probabilistic trade-off**. Specifically, Bloom filters may produce **false positives**, meaning they may incorrectly report that an element is in the set when it is not. However, **false negatives** are not possible; if an element is not in the set, the Bloom filter will correctly report that it is not.

False Positive Probability:

The probability of a **false positive** (i.e., reporting an element as a member when it is not) depends on two factors:

1. **Size of the Bit Array (m):** The larger the bit array, the fewer collisions occur, reducing the likelihood of false positives.
2. **Number of Hash Functions (k):** The more hash functions you use, the more bits are set in the array, increasing the likelihood of collisions, which can also increase the false positive probability.

The false positive probability, **P(fps)**, can be estimated by the formula:

P(fps)≈(1−e−k·nm)kP(fps) \approx \left(1 - e^{-\frac{k \cdot n}{m}}\right)^kP(fps)≈(1−e−mk·n)k

Where:

- **n** is the number of elements inserted into the Bloom filter.
- **m** is the size of the bit array.
- **k** is the number of hash functions.

163

Trade-offs:

- **Time vs. Space:** By increasing the size of the bit array (m) and the number of hash functions (k), you reduce the probability of false positives but at the cost of increased space (more memory) and time (more hash function evaluations per operation).
- **Space Efficiency:** Bloom filters provide highly space-efficient solutions, but the trade-off is that they allow for false positives. The goal is to minimize the false positive rate while maintaining a small bit array and a manageable number of hash functions.

Example:

Let's say we have a Bloom filter with a bit array size of 1,000 bits and we're using 3 hash functions. If we insert 100 elements into the filter, the false positive probability can be computed using the formula above. By adjusting the parameters (bit array size and number of hash functions), we can tune the Bloom filter's performance to balance memory usage and error rates.

Real-World Examples: Bloom Filters in Web Caching and Spam Detection

Bloom filters are used in various real-world applications where space efficiency and fast membership testing are critical. Let's explore two such examples: **web caching** and **spam detection**.

1. Web Caching:

Web caching involves storing copies of frequently accessed web pages, images, or other resources to reduce load times and server requests. A common use of Bloom filters in caching is to test whether a resource is already cached without having to look up the entire cache.

- **Problem:** In a web cache, we often need to check if a requested resource is in the cache before fetching it from the server. This check should be fast, especially for large caches.
- **Solution with Bloom Filters:**
  - A Bloom filter is used to test whether the requested resource is in the cache. The Bloom filter stores a probabilistic representation of all cached URLs or resource keys.
  - When a user requests a resource, the Bloom filter quickly checks if the resource is in the cache. If the Bloom filter says "no," the resource is definitely not in the cache. If the Bloom filter says "yes," the resource might be in the cache, so the

system proceeds to check the actual cache (which may incur a performance hit).

o The Bloom filter speeds up the process, reducing the time spent checking whether the resource is cached.

2. Spam Detection:

Spam filters aim to identify and block unwanted or malicious emails. One way to efficiently check if an email or URL is part of a known spam list is by using a Bloom filter.

- **Problem:** With millions of spam emails and URLs to check, searching for each element in a traditional data structure like a hash set would be too slow and memory-intensive.
- **Solution with Bloom Filters:**
  o A Bloom filter can be used to represent a list of known spam words, email addresses, or URLs. As each new email or URL is processed, it is checked against the Bloom filter to see if it matches any known spam entries.
  o If the Bloom filter returns "no," the email is definitely not spam. If the Bloom filter returns "yes," there is a possibility that the email is spam, and further checks can be done.

o   This probabilistic approach allows the spam filter to work quickly, using much less memory than storing the entire spam list.

Conclusion

In this chapter, we explored **Bloom filters**, a **space-efficient probabilistic data structure** used for fast **set membership testing**. We discussed:

- **How Bloom filters work** by using a bit array and multiple hash functions.
- The **false positive probability** and the trade-off between time complexity, space efficiency, and error rates.
- **Real-world applications** of Bloom filters, including **web caching** and **spam detection**, where their speed and efficiency provide significant performance benefits.

Bloom filters are an invaluable tool for situations where memory is limited and approximate results are acceptable. In the next chapter, we will delve into **cache coherence protocols** in distributed systems, an important topic in ensuring consistency and synchronization across multiple machines in a network.

CHAPTER 16

GRAPHS: REPRESENTING COMPLEX RELATIONSHIPS

Graphs are one of the most fundamental and versatile data structures used in computer science. They are used to model **complex relationships** between entities, where the entities are represented by **vertices** (or nodes) and the relationships between them are represented by **edges** (or links). Graphs are used in a wide range of applications, from representing networks like the **Internet** to modeling complex systems in fields like biology, transportation, and social media.

In this chapter, we will:

- Cover the **basics of graph theory**, including the concepts of **vertices**, **edges**, and the difference between **directed** and **undirected graphs**.
- Discuss the two most common **graph representations**: the **adjacency list** and the **adjacency matrix**.
- Explore **real-world examples** of graphs, such as **social networks**, **web pages**, and **routing problems**, where graphs are used to represent relationships and solve problems.

168

Basic Graph Theory: Vertices, Edges, Directed vs. Undirected Graphs

A **graph** consists of a set of **vertices** (also called **nodes**) and a set of **edges** (also called **arcs**) that connect pairs of vertices.

1. Vertices and Edges:

- **Vertices (Nodes):** A vertex represents an entity in the graph. For example, in a social network graph, each vertex might represent a user.
- **Edges (Links):** An edge represents a relationship or connection between two vertices. In the social network example, an edge could represent a "friendship" or a "follow" relationship between two users.

2. Directed vs. Undirected Graphs:

- **Directed Graph (Digraph):** In a directed graph, the edges have a direction, meaning they point from one vertex to another. This is often used to represent relationships where direction matters.
  - o **Example:** A **Twitter** follower graph is directed, as a user may follow someone, but the reverse is not necessarily true.

169

- **Undirected Graph:** In an undirected graph, the edges have no direction, meaning the relationship is bidirectional. An edge between two vertices signifies a mutual connection.
  - o **Example:** A **Facebook** friendship graph is undirected because if one user is friends with another, the relationship is mutual.

3. Weighted vs. Unweighted Graphs:

- **Weighted Graphs:** In weighted graphs, edges have associated weights (or costs), which can represent things like distance, time, or cost to travel between nodes.
  - o **Example:** A **road network** where the edges represent roads between cities and the weights represent the distances or travel times.
- **Unweighted Graphs:** In unweighted graphs, all edges are considered equal, meaning no weights are associated with them.
  - o **Example:** A **social network** where all friendships are treated equally, and there's no additional cost or weight associated with the relationship.

Graph Representations: Adjacency List vs. Adjacency Matrix

Graphs can be represented in various ways depending on the application and the required operations. Two of the most common representations are the **adjacency list** and the **adjacency matrix**.

1. Adjacency List:

An **adjacency list** is a collection of lists or arrays, where each vertex has a list of adjacent vertices (i.e., the vertices it is directly connected to by edges). This representation is space-efficient for sparse graphs (graphs with relatively few edges compared to vertices).

- **Representation:**
  - o For an undirected graph, if there's an edge between vertex A and vertex B, both A and B will appear in each other's adjacency lists.
  - o For a directed graph, the adjacency list for a vertex will only contain the vertices that the vertex points to.
- **Example:** For the following undirected graph:

```
less

A -- B
|    |
```

```
C -- D
```

The adjacency list representation would look like this:

```
mathematica
```

```
A: [B, C]
B: [A, D]
C: [A, D]
D: [B, C]
```

In this case:

- Vertex A is connected to vertices B and C.
- Vertex B is connected to vertices A and D.
- Vertex C is connected to vertices A and D.
- Vertex D is connected to vertices B and C.

2. Adjacency Matrix:

An **adjacency matrix** is a 2D array (or matrix) where each element at position (i, j) represents the presence or weight of an edge between vertex i and vertex j. This representation is often used for dense graphs (graphs with many edges) but can be inefficient for sparse graphs because it uses a lot of memory.

- **Representation:**
  - In an undirected graph, the matrix is symmetric, meaning matrix[i][j] = matrix[j][i].

172

- o In a directed graph, the matrix is not necessarily symmetric.
- o If the graph is weighted, the matrix entries contain the weights of the edges, otherwise, they can be 1 (for presence) or 0 (for absence).
- **Example:** For the same undirected graph:

```less
A -- B
|    |
C -- D
```

The adjacency matrix representation would look like this:

```css
    A  B  C  D
A   0  1  1  0
B   1  0  0  1
C   1  0  0  1
D   0  1  1  0
```

Here, the rows and columns represent the vertices, and the 1s indicate an edge between two vertices.

Comparing the Two Representations:

- **Adjacency List:**

173

- o **Space Complexity:** O(V + E), where V is the number of vertices and E is the number of edges.
- o **Time Complexity for Operations:**
  - Searching for neighbors: O(degree of vertex) = O(E/V) on average.
  - Insertion: O(1) for each edge.
- **Adjacency Matrix:**
  - o **Space Complexity:** O(V²), regardless of the number of edges.
  - o **Time Complexity for Operations:**
    - Searching for neighbors: O(1).
    - Insertion: O(1) for each edge.

The adjacency matrix is better suited for dense graphs where E is close to V², while the adjacency list is better for sparse graphs.

Real-World Example: Representing Social Networks, Web Pages, and Routing Problems

Graphs are used to represent a wide variety of systems in the real world. Below are a few key examples of how graphs are applied in practice.

1. Representing Social Networks:

In social networks (like Facebook or Twitter), **vertices** represent users, and **edges** represent relationships such as friendships or followers.

- **Undirected Graphs:** A friendship in a social network is usually represented as an undirected edge, as it is typically mutual.
- **Directed Graphs:** In a platform like Twitter, the relationship between users can be represented by a directed graph, where a directed edge from A to B means that user A follows user B, but not necessarily the other way around.

Example:

In a social network, if user A is friends with users B and C, and B is friends with C, the graph can be represented as:

```
less


A -- B
|    |
C -- D
```

This structure can be represented using either an adjacency list or an adjacency matrix, depending on the needs of the application.

2. Web Pages and Hyperlinks:

The **World Wide Web** is another example where graphs are used to represent relationships. In this case:

- **Vertices** represent **web pages**.
- **Edges** represent **hyperlinks** between pages.

The web is often modeled as a **directed graph** since a hyperlink from one page to another doesn't necessarily imply a reverse link.

3. Routing Problems:

In **network routing** or **transportation systems**, graphs are used to represent routes between locations.

- **Vertices** represent **cities** or **network nodes**.
- **Edges** represent the **routes** between these cities or nodes, with weights representing travel times, distances, or costs.

Graph algorithms like **Dijkstra's algorithm** (for shortest paths) and **Bellman-Ford algorithm** rely on efficient graph representations to calculate the most efficient route.

Example:

In a transportation network, a graph can be used to find the shortest path from city A to city D:

```
less

A --5-- B --2-- D
|       |
3       1
|
C
```

This graph could be represented using an adjacency list or matrix, and an algorithm like **Dijkstra's** would help find the shortest path from A to D.

Conclusion

In this chapter, we explored **graphs**, a powerful data structure used to represent and solve problems involving relationships and connectivity. We covered:

- **Basic graph theory** concepts such as **vertices, edges**, and the difference between **directed** and **undirected graphs**.
- **Graph representations**, specifically the **adjacency list** and **adjacency matrix**, and when each is preferred based on graph density.
- **Real-world examples** of graphs in **social networks, web pages**, and **routing problems**, showcasing how graphs

are used to model complex systems and solve practical problems.

Graphs are fundamental to understanding networks, relationships, and paths, and they are used in numerous fields such as computer science, telecommunications, transportation, and social sciences. In the next chapter, we will explore **graph algorithms**, diving into algorithms for searching, traversal, shortest path finding, and more.

CHAPTER 17

DEPTH-FIRST SEARCH (DFS) AND BREADTH-FIRST SEARCH (BFS)

Graph traversal is a fundamental operation in computer science and is used in many different applications, such as searching, finding paths, or exploring networks. Two of the most widely used algorithms for graph traversal are **Depth-First Search (DFS)** and **Breadth-First Search (BFS)**. These algorithms allow us to systematically visit all the vertices of a graph in a particular order.

In this chapter, we will:

- Understand the **DFS** and **BFS** algorithms and how they traverse graphs.
- Discuss the **time** and **space complexities** of both DFS and BFS.
- Explore **real-world use cases** of these algorithms, such as finding **shortest paths** and **network exploration**.

Understanding DFS and BFS Algorithms for Graph Traversal

Both **Depth-First Search (DFS)** and **Breadth-First Search (BFS)** are algorithms used to explore a graph. However, they differ significantly in how they traverse the graph and the order in which they visit the vertices.

1. Depth-First Search (DFS):

DFS is an algorithm for traversing or searching through a graph. It starts at the root (or any arbitrary node in the graph) and explores as far as possible along each branch before backtracking. This means that DFS explores a node's descendants before visiting the node's neighbors at the same level.

How DFS Works:

- Start at the root (or any arbitrary node).
- Explore as far as possible along a path by visiting an adjacent vertex.
- If you reach a vertex that has no unvisited neighbors, backtrack to the previous vertex and continue exploring the other branches.
- Repeat this process until all nodes have been visited.

DFS is typically implemented using a **recursive approach** or with an explicit **stack**.

DFS Algorithm (Pseudocode):

scss

```
DFS(graph, vertex):
    if vertex is not visited:
        mark vertex as visited
        for each neighbor of vertex:
            DFS(graph, neighbor)
```

2. Breadth-First Search (BFS):

BFS is an algorithm for traversing or searching through a graph where you start at the root (or any arbitrary node) and explore all the neighbors at the current level before moving on to the next level. This means BFS explores all vertices at the present depth level before moving on to vertices at the next depth level.

How BFS Works:

- Start at the root (or any arbitrary node).
- Explore all its neighbors first, then move to the neighbors' neighbors.
- Continue this process, level by level, until all nodes are visited.
- BFS is typically implemented using a **queue** to keep track of the nodes to be visited.

BFS Algorithm (Pseudocode):

vbnet

```
BFS(graph, start_vertex):
    create a queue
    enqueue start_vertex
    mark start_vertex as visited
    while queue is not empty:
        vertex = dequeue from queue
        for each neighbor of vertex:
            if neighbor is not visited:
                mark neighbor as visited
                enqueue neighbor
```

Time and Space Complexities of DFS and BFS

Both DFS and BFS are **graph traversal algorithms**, and their time and space complexities are quite similar. However, there are subtle differences in their implementations and use cases that affect their performance.

1. Time Complexity:

- **DFS:**
    - **Time Complexity: O(V + E)**, where V is the number of vertices and E is the number of edges.

182

- o In the worst case, we must visit every vertex and edge once.

- **BFS:**
  - o **Time Complexity: O(V + E)**, where V is the number of vertices and E is the number of edges.
  - o Like DFS, BFS must visit each vertex and edge once.

2. Space Complexity:

- **DFS:**
  - o **Space Complexity: O(V)**, where V is the number of vertices.
  - o This is because DFS requires a stack to remember which nodes to visit next, and the stack can grow to the size of the graph's vertices in the worst case (e.g., in case of a long path).
- **BFS:**
  - o **Space Complexity: O(V)**, where V is the number of vertices.
  - o BFS uses a queue to keep track of vertices at the current level, and the queue may hold all the vertices at a level (which, in the worst case, can be all the vertices).

Key Differences:

- **DFS** has a **deeper exploration** strategy and uses **less memory in sparse graphs** because it only stores one branch of the graph at a time.
- **BFS** has a **broader exploration** strategy and may use more memory in dense graphs, as it stores all the nodes at the current level in the queue.

Real-World Use Cases: Finding Shortest Paths, Network Exploration

Both DFS and BFS are used extensively in real-world applications, particularly for tasks that involve **searching**, **pathfinding**, and **network exploration**.

1. Finding Shortest Paths (BFS):

BFS is particularly useful when finding the **shortest path** in an **unweighted graph**. The reason BFS works well is that it explores all nodes at the present depth before moving on to nodes at the next depth level, ensuring that the first time we encounter a node, we have found the shortest path to it.

Example: Shortest Path in an Unweighted Graph

Consider the following graph:

mathematica

```
A -- B -- C
|         |
D -- E -- F
```

- Starting from vertex A, BFS will explore level by level, ensuring that the shortest path from A to any vertex is found first.
- **Time Complexity for BFS (Shortest Path): O(V + E)**, where V is the number of vertices and E is the number of edges. This is because BFS visits each vertex and edge exactly once.

BFS is commonly used in **web crawling**, **social network analysis**, and **routing algorithms** to find the shortest path or connection between nodes.

2. Network Exploration (DFS and BFS):

Both DFS and BFS are used for **network exploration** to find connected components in a network or identify relationships between nodes.

- **DFS for Network Exploration:**

185

- o DFS is ideal for exploring all reachable nodes from a given starting node, making it suitable for identifying **strongly connected components** or searching through a tree-like structure.

- o Example: In a **network topology** (such as a computer network), DFS can help in exploring all nodes connected to a specific node.

- **BFS for Network Exploration:**
  - o BFS is often used in **broadcasting** or **message propagation** in networks. It can be used to model the spread of information or viruses in a network by exploring neighbors level by level.

  - o Example: **Packet routing** in computer networks, where BFS helps find the shortest path for packets to reach their destination node.

3. Solving Maze Problems (DFS and BFS):

Both DFS and BFS can be used to solve maze problems, where the goal is to find a path from a starting point to a goal point.

- **DFS for Mazes:**
  - o DFS explores paths deeply and can be used to **find a path** from start to goal. However, it may explore suboptimal paths first.

  - o DFS is typically used in **backtracking algorithms** for maze-solving problems.

- **BFS for Mazes:**
  - o BFS is often preferred in maze-solving problems if the goal is to **find the shortest path**. Since BFS explores all nodes at the current depth before moving on to the next, it ensures the shortest path is found first.

Example: Implementing DFS and BFS for Graph Traversal

Let's implement both **DFS** and **BFS** for a simple graph represented as an adjacency list.

```python
# Graph Representation (Adjacency List)
graph = {
    'A': ['B', 'D'],
    'B': ['A', 'C'],
    'C': ['B', 'F'],
    'D': ['A', 'E'],
    'E': ['D', 'F'],
    'F': ['C', 'E']
}

# DFS Implementation
```

187

```python
def dfs(graph, start, visited=None):
    if visited is None:
        visited = set()
    visited.add(start)
    print(start, end=" ")

    for neighbor in graph[start]:
        if neighbor not in visited:
            dfs(graph, neighbor, visited)

# BFS Implementation
from collections import deque

def bfs(graph, start):
    visited = set()
    queue = deque([start])
    visited.add(start)

    while queue:
        vertex = queue.popleft()
        print(vertex, end=" ")

        for neighbor in graph[vertex]:
            if neighbor not in visited:
                visited.add(neighbor)
                queue.append(neighbor)

# Example Usage
print("DFS traversal:")
```

```
dfs(graph, 'A')

print("\nBFS traversal:")
bfs(graph, 'A')
```

Explanation:

- **DFS:** The `dfs()` function uses recursion to explore each vertex's neighbors and continues until all reachable vertices are visited. We use a set `visited` to keep track of visited vertices.
- **BFS:** The `bfs()` function uses a queue to explore the graph level by level, ensuring that vertices are visited in the shortest-path order.

Output:

```
mathematica
```

```
DFS traversal:
A B C F E D
```

```
BFS traversal:
A B D C F E
```

In this example, DFS explores as deep as possible before backtracking, whereas BFS explores all neighbors level by level.

Conclusion

In this chapter, we explored **Depth-First Search (DFS)** and **Breadth-First Search (BFS)**, two fundamental algorithms for graph traversal. We discussed their differences in terms of their approach to exploring a graph and their **time** and **space complexities**.

DFS is ideal for exploring deeper into the graph, while BFS is better suited for finding the **shortest paths** in an unweighted graph. Both algorithms are widely used in real-world applications, such as **network exploration, shortest path finding**, and **maze-solving**.

Understanding DFS and BFS is crucial for solving many graph-related problems efficiently, and in the next chapter, we will explore more advanced **graph algorithms** like **Dijkstra's algorithm** for weighted graphs and **Kruskal's algorithm** for finding the minimum spanning tree.

CHAPTER 18

SHORTEST PATH ALGORITHMS: DIJKSTRA AND BELLMAN-FORD

Finding the **shortest path** between two points is one of the most fundamental problems in graph theory. Whether it's routing data across a network, planning the best route in GPS systems, or minimizing costs in logistics, **shortest path algorithms** are widely used in various real-world applications. Two of the most well-known algorithms for finding the shortest path in a **weighted graph** are **Dijkstra's algorithm** and the **Bellman-Ford algorithm**.

In this chapter, we will:

- Provide an **overview of Dijkstra's algorithm**, which is used to find the shortest path in graphs with non-negative weights.
- Explore the **Bellman-Ford algorithm**, which handles negative edge weights and can detect negative weight cycles.
- Discuss **real-world applications**, such as **GPS routing** and **network routing protocols**, where shortest path algorithms are heavily used.

Overview of Dijkstra's Algorithm for Shortest Paths in Weighted Graphs

Dijkstra's algorithm is a **greedy algorithm** that finds the shortest path from a source vertex to all other vertices in a **weighted graph** with **non-negative edge weights**. It works by iteratively choosing the vertex with the smallest tentative distance and exploring its neighbors.

How Dijkstra's Algorithm Works:

1. **Initialization:**
   - o Assign an initial distance of 0 to the source vertex and infinity to all other vertices.
   - o Mark all vertices as unvisited.
2. **Visit the Nearest Unvisited Vertex:**
   - o Select the unvisited vertex with the smallest known distance (tentative distance). Initially, this will be the source vertex.
3. **Update Tentative Distances:**
   - o For each neighbor of the selected vertex, calculate the tentative distance from the source through this vertex. If the calculated distance is smaller than the current known distance, update it.

4. **Mark the Vertex as Visited:**

   o   Once all the neighbors of the current vertex are processed, mark the vertex as visited. A visited vertex will not be checked again.

5. **Repeat:**

   o   Repeat steps 2–4 until all vertices have been visited or the shortest path to all vertices has been determined.

Dijkstra's Algorithm (Pseudocode):

arduino

```
Dijkstra(graph, source):
    dist[source] = 0
    for each vertex v in graph:
        if v != source:
            dist[v] = ∞
        prev[v] = undefined

    priority_queue = create_priority_queue()
    priority_queue.insert(source, dist[source])

    while priority_queue is not empty:
        u = priority_queue.extract_min()
        for each neighbor v of u:
            alt = dist[u] + weight(u, v)
            if alt < dist[v]:
                dist[v] = alt
                prev[v] = u
```

193

```
            priority_queue.insert(v,
dist[v])
```

```
    return dist, prev
```

Time Complexity:

- **O(V²)** for the naive implementation (using an array).
- **O((V + E) log V)** with a priority queue (using a min-heap), where V is the number of vertices and E is the number of edges.

Dijkstra's algorithm is efficient for graphs with **non-negative edge weights**, but it does not work with graphs containing negative weights.

Bellman-Ford Algorithm and Its Ability to Handle Negative Weights

The **Bellman-Ford algorithm** is another algorithm used to find the shortest path from a source vertex to all other vertices, but it has an important advantage: it can handle **negative edge weights** and can also detect **negative weight cycles**.

How Bellman-Ford Algorithm Works:

1. **Initialization:**

194

- o Like Dijkstra, set the distance to the source vertex as 0 and the distance to all other vertices as infinity.

2. **Relaxation:**
   - o For each vertex, iterate through all edges and relax them by updating the distance to the neighboring vertex if a shorter path is found.

3. **Repeat Relaxation:**
   - o Perform the relaxation step **V-1 times**, where v is the number of vertices. This ensures that the shortest path is found.

4. **Check for Negative Weight Cycles:**
   - o After the relaxation, if you can still relax any edge, it indicates that there is a **negative weight cycle** in the graph.

Bellman-Ford Algorithm (Pseudocode):

bash

```
BellmanFord(graph, source):
    dist[source] = 0
    for each vertex v in graph:
        if v != source:
            dist[v] = ∞

    for i = 1 to V-1:  # Relax all edges V-1 times
        for each edge (u, v) with weight w:
            if dist[u] + w < dist[v]:
```

```
        dist[v] = dist[u] + w

    # Check for negative-weight cycles
    for each edge (u, v) with weight w:
        if dist[u] + w < dist[v]:
            return "Graph contains negative
weight cycle"

    return dist
```

Time Complexity:

- **O(V * E)**, where V is the number of vertices and E is the number of edges. This is because the relaxation step takes **O(E)** time, and we repeat it **V-1 times**.

Bellman-Ford is slower than Dijkstra's algorithm but is useful in graphs with **negative edge weights**. It also has the added feature of detecting negative weight cycles.

Real-World Use Case: Routing in GPS and Network Routing Protocols

Shortest path algorithms like **Dijkstra's** and **Bellman-Ford** are crucial in **routing algorithms** used in **GPS systems** and **network routing protocols**. Let's explore how these algorithms are applied in real-world scenarios:

196

1. GPS Routing (Dijkstra's Algorithm):

In **GPS navigation systems**, the goal is to find the shortest route between two locations based on the road network. The road network can be modeled as a **weighted graph**, where the vertices represent locations (cities, intersections) and the edges represent roads with weights corresponding to the travel time, distance, or cost.

- **Dijkstra's algorithm** is typically used to find the **shortest path** between the current location and the destination because it can efficiently handle graphs with **non-negative weights**, such as time or distance between intersections.
- **Example:** Given a set of cities and roads between them, Dijkstra's algorithm helps to find the fastest or most optimal route from the starting city to the destination, based on factors like distance or estimated travel time.

2. Network Routing (Bellman-Ford and Dijkstra's Algorithm):

In **network routing**, the goal is to route data packets between nodes (routers, switches) in a communication network. These networks are often represented as **graphs**, where nodes represent routers or switches, and edges represent network links with associated weights (such as bandwidth, latency, or cost).

- **Dijkstra's algorithm** is often used in **link-state routing protocols** (e.g., **OSPF** - Open Shortest Path First) to calculate the shortest path from a router to all other routers in the network.

- **Bellman-Ford** is used in **distance-vector routing protocols** (e.g., **RIP** - Routing Information Protocol), where each router maintains a table of shortest paths to all other routers and exchanges this information with neighboring routers. Bellman-Ford is also used here due to its ability to handle negative weights, which could occur due to varying network conditions.

- **Example:** In a large-scale network, Bellman-Ford or Dijkstra's algorithm helps routers calculate the optimal route for data transmission, ensuring that data packets take the most efficient path while minimizing latency or packet loss.

Example: Implementing Dijkstra's and Bellman-Ford Algorithms

Let's implement both **Dijkstra's algorithm** and **Bellman-Ford algorithm** for finding the shortest paths in a graph.

```
python
```

198

```python
import heapq

# Dijkstra's Algorithm
def dijkstra(graph, start):
    # Initialize distances and priority queue
    dist = {vertex: float('inf') for vertex in graph}
    dist[start] = 0
    priority_queue = [(0, start)]  # (distance, vertex)

    while priority_queue:
        current_distance, current_vertex = heapq.heappop(priority_queue)

        if current_distance > dist[current_vertex]:
            continue

        for neighbor, weight in graph[current_vertex]:
            distance = current_distance + weight
            if distance < dist[neighbor]:
                dist[neighbor] = distance
                heapq.heappush(priority_queue, (distance, neighbor))

    return dist
```

```python
# Bellman-Ford Algorithm
def bellman_ford(graph, start):
    dist = {vertex: float('inf') for vertex in graph}
    dist[start] = 0

    # Relax edges V-1 times
    for _ in range(len(graph) - 1):
        for vertex in graph:
            for neighbor, weight in graph[vertex]:
                if dist[vertex] + weight < dist[neighbor]:
                    dist[neighbor] = dist[vertex] + weight

    # Check for negative weight cycles
    for vertex in graph:
        for neighbor, weight in graph[vertex]:
            if dist[vertex] + weight < dist[neighbor]:
                return "Graph contains negative weight cycle"

    return dist

# Example graph (directed and weighted)
graph = {
    'A': [('B', 1), ('C', 4)],
```

```
    'B': [('C', 2), ('D', 5)],
    'C': [('D', 1)],
    'D': []
}


# Dijkstra's Algorithm Output
print("Dijkstra's  Algorithm:",  dijkstra(graph,
'A'))


# Bellman-Ford Algorithm Output
print("Bellman-Ford              Algorithm:",
bellman_ford(graph, 'A'))
```

Explanation:

- **Dijkstra's Algorithm:** We use a **priority queue** (min-heap) to always select the vertex with the smallest known distance, and we update the distances to neighboring vertices accordingly.
- **Bellman-Ford Algorithm:** We relax all edges **V-1 times** (where V is the number of vertices) and check for negative weight cycles after the relaxation.

Conclusion

In this chapter, we explored two key algorithms for finding the **shortest path** in weighted graphs: **Dijkstra's algorithm** and **Bellman-Ford algorithm**. We covered:

- **Dijkstra's algorithm**, which is efficient for graphs with **non-negative edge weights** and is used in applications like **GPS routing** and **network routing**.
- **Bellman-Ford algorithm**, which can handle **negative edge weights** and is used in **distance-vector routing protocols**.

Both algorithms are essential tools in **graph theory** and are widely used in real-world applications like **network routing**, **shortest path calculation**, and **routing protocols** in distributed systems. In the next chapter, we will delve into **minimum spanning tree algorithms** like **Prim's algorithm** and **Kruskal's algorithm**.

CHAPTER 19

FLOYD-WARSHALL ALGORITHM: ALL-PAIRS SHORTEST PATH

When working with graphs, there are cases where we need to find the **shortest paths between all pairs of vertices**, rather than just between a single source and a destination. For these scenarios, the **Floyd-Warshall algorithm** provides a powerful solution by computing the shortest paths between every pair of vertices in a weighted graph.

In this chapter, we will:

- Introduce the **Floyd-Warshall algorithm** and explain how it computes the shortest paths between all pairs of vertices.

- Discuss the **matrix-based implementation** of the algorithm and analyze its **time complexity**.

- Explore **real-world applications**, such as **traffic modeling** and **network analysis**, where the Floyd-Warshall algorithm can be used to solve shortest path problems in **dense networks**.

Introduction to the Floyd-Warshall Algorithm for Finding All Pairs of Shortest Paths

The **Floyd-Warshall algorithm** is an **all-pairs shortest path algorithm** that finds the shortest paths between every pair of vertices in a graph. Unlike **Dijkstra's algorithm** and **Bellman-Ford algorithm**, which find the shortest path from a single source to all other vertices, the Floyd-Warshall algorithm computes the shortest paths between all pairs of vertices simultaneously.

Algorithm Overview:

The Floyd-Warshall algorithm uses **dynamic programming** to iteratively improve the estimate of the shortest path between two vertices. It starts by assuming that the shortest path between any two vertices is the direct edge between them. Then, it considers whether introducing an intermediate vertex between the two vertices provides a shorter path.

The algorithm works in **3 nested loops**:

1. Loop over each possible intermediate vertex.
2. For each pair of vertices, check if the shortest path can be improved by passing through the intermediate vertex.
3. Update the distance matrix with the new shortest paths.

Floyd-Warshall Algorithm (Pseudocode):

yaml

```
FloydWarshall(graph):
    let dist be a 2D array of size VxV, where
dist[i][j] is the shortest distance from vertex
i to vertex j
    for each vertex v:
        dist[v][v] = 0  # Distance to itself is
0
    for each edge (u, v) with weight w:
        dist[u][v] = w  # Initialize distances
for direct edges

    for k = 0 to V-1:  # Iterate through all
vertices as intermediate vertices
        for i = 0 to V-1:  # Iterate through all
source vertices
            for j = 0 to V-1:  # Iterate through
all destination vertices
                if dist[i][j] > dist[i][k] +
dist[k][j]:
                    dist[i][j] = dist[i][k] +
dist[k][j]

    return dist  # The dist matrix now contains
the shortest paths between all pairs of vertices
```

In this pseudocode:

- **dist[i][j]** represents the shortest path from vertex i to vertex j.
- Initially, the distance between vertices is set to the direct edge weight, and the distance between two unconnected vertices is set to infinity.
- The algorithm iterates through all vertices as **intermediate vertices**, checking if using an intermediate vertex improves the shortest path between any two vertices.

Matrix-Based Implementation and Its Time Complexity

The Floyd-Warshall algorithm is often implemented using a **distance matrix**. This matrix stores the shortest distance between all pairs of vertices. The algorithm updates this matrix iteratively to find the shortest paths between all pairs.

Matrix Representation:

The matrix dist is initialized with:

- **dist[i][j]** = ∞ for all pairs (i, j) where there is no direct edge between i and j.
- **dist[i][j]** = **w** for each direct edge (i, j) with weight w.

- **dist[i][i]** = **0** for all vertices i, as the distance from a vertex to itself is 0.

The Floyd-Warshall algorithm has three nested loops:

- The outer loop runs **V** times (where v is the number of vertices) for each possible intermediate vertex.
- The two inner loops iterate over all pairs of vertices, so they each run **V** times as well.

Thus, the overall time complexity of the Floyd-Warshall algorithm is:

$O(V3)O(V^3)O(V3)$

This makes the algorithm efficient for **dense graphs** (graphs with many edges), but less efficient for **sparse graphs**. For graphs with a large number of vertices, the cubic time complexity can become a bottleneck.

The space complexity of the algorithm is:

$O(V2)O(V^2)O(V2)$

This is due to the storage of the **distance matrix** `dist`, which requires space for all pairs of vertices.

Real-World Applications: Shortest Path Problems in Dense Networks and Traffic Modeling

The Floyd-Warshall algorithm is particularly useful for solving **all-pairs shortest path problems**, where you need to compute the shortest path between all pairs of vertices in a graph. This makes it ideal for applications where the graph is relatively **dense**, or where you need to compute shortest paths in **large networks**.

1. Traffic Modeling:

In **traffic networks**, roads and intersections can be modeled as a graph where:

- **Vertices** represent intersections or cities.
- **Edges** represent roads, with weights corresponding to travel time, distance, or traffic congestion.

The Floyd-Warshall algorithm can be used to compute the **shortest travel times** between all pairs of intersections or cities. This information can be used to optimize traffic flow, improve route planning, or analyze congestion patterns.

- **Example:** Given a city with a network of roads, the Floyd-Warshall algorithm can be used by traffic management systems to calculate the shortest travel times between all pairs of intersections, which helps in providing real-time traffic updates and efficient routing suggestions.

2. Dense Network Routing:

In **telecommunication networks** or **data networks**, routers and switches are connected by various communication links, and finding the optimal route for data packets is crucial to ensure efficient data transmission. The Floyd-Warshall algorithm can be applied to compute the shortest paths between all pairs of nodes in a **dense network**.

- **Example:** In a **telecom network**, where each router is connected to many others, the Floyd-Warshall algorithm can be used to compute the shortest paths between every pair of routers, enabling efficient routing decisions for data packets.

3. Finding All Shortest Paths in a Graph:

In **web crawling**, **search engines**, and **social network analysis**, it is often necessary to find the shortest path between all pairs of nodes. For example, in a social network, you may want to calculate the **shortest distance** between all pairs of users to identify relationships or communities.

- **Example:** In **social networks**, the Floyd-Warshall algorithm can be used to find the shortest path between all pairs of users, helping to identify **friendship distances** and **social clusters**.

Example: Implementing Floyd-Warshall Algorithm

Here is a Python implementation of the **Floyd-Warshall algorithm** to compute the shortest paths between all pairs of vertices in a weighted graph:

python

```
# Floyd-Warshall Algorithm Implementation
def floyd_warshall(graph):
    # Initialize the distance matrix with graph
weights
    V = len(graph)
    dist = [[float('inf')] * V for _ in range(V)]

    # Set the distance of a vertex to itself as
0
```

```
    for i in range(V):
        dist[i][i] = 0

    # Set initial distances from the graph's
edges
    for u in range(V):
        for v, weight in graph[u]:
            dist[u][v] = weight

    # Apply the Floyd-Warshall algorithm
    for k in range(V):  # Intermediate vertex
        for i in range(V):  # Source vertex
            for j in range(V):  # Destination
vertex
                if dist[i][j] > dist[i][k] +
dist[k][j]:
                    dist[i][j] = dist[i][k] +
dist[k][j]

    return dist

# Example graph: adjacency list representation
graph = {
    0: [(1, 5), (2, 9), (3, 10)],
    1: [(2, 3)],
    2: [(3, 1)],
    3: []
}
```

```
# Compute shortest paths using Floyd-Warshall
shortest_paths = floyd_warshall(graph)

# Display shortest paths between all pairs of
vertices
for row in shortest_paths:
    print(row)
```

Explanation:

- The graph is represented using an adjacency list, where each vertex points to a list of tuples representing the neighbors and their edge weights.
- The `floyd_warshall` function initializes the `dist` matrix with distances from the graph's edges, then updates it iteratively by considering every vertex as an intermediate vertex.
- The result is a matrix where `dist[i][j]` represents the shortest path from vertex `i` to vertex `j`.

Output:

css

```
[0, 5, 8, 9]
[∞, 0, 3, 4]
[∞, ∞, 0, 1]
[∞, ∞, ∞, 0]
```

In this example:

212

- The shortest path from vertex 0 to vertex 1 is 5, from 0 to 2 is 8, and from 0 to 3 is 9, etc.

Conclusion

In this chapter, we explored the **Floyd-Warshall algorithm**, an efficient method for computing the **all-pairs shortest paths** in a graph. We learned about:

- The **matrix-based implementation** of the algorithm and its $O(V^3)$ time complexity, which makes it well-suited for **dense graphs**.
- **Real-world applications** in **traffic modeling, network routing**, and **social network analysis**, where calculating the shortest paths between all pairs of nodes is essential.

The Floyd-Warshall algorithm is a fundamental algorithm for handling **dense networks** and situations where the shortest path between any pair of vertices is required. In the next chapter, we will explore **minimum spanning tree algorithms**, such as **Prim's** and **Kruskal's** algorithms, which are used to find the least-cost tree that spans all vertices in a graph.

CHAPTER 20:

A *ALGORITHM*: OPTIMIZED PATH FINDING

When it comes to pathfinding in graphs, especially in **games** or **AI simulations**, the need for an **efficient** and **optimal** algorithm to find the shortest path is critical. While algorithms like **Dijkstra's** are excellent for finding the shortest path, they can be inefficient in certain cases where we only care about reaching a destination as quickly as possible. This is where the **A*** (A-star) algorithm shines.

In this chapter, we will:

- Introduce the **A*** algorithm and explain how it uses a **heuristic-driven approach** to optimize pathfinding.
- Discuss how **A*** differs from **Dijkstra's algorithm** in terms of efficiency and application.
- Explore **real-world applications**, particularly in **games** for **NPC pathfinding** and **AI simulations**.

214

A Algorithm and Its Heuristic-Driven Approach to Pathfinding*

The **A*** algorithm is a **graph traversal** and **pathfinding algorithm** that is widely used for finding the shortest path between two nodes in a graph. What makes **A*** unique is its ability to optimize the search process by using a **heuristic function** in addition to the cost of the path already traveled. This makes A* more efficient than other algorithms like Dijkstra's, especially in cases where we need to navigate large, complex graphs.

Key Components of the A Algorithm:*

The **A*** algorithm relies on the following components:

1. **g(n):** The actual cost from the start node to the current node n. This is the **cost so far**.
2. **h(n):** The heuristic estimate of the cost from node n to the goal. This is the **estimated cost to reach the goal** from n.
3. **f(n):** The total cost function, which combines both the actual cost and the heuristic. It is defined as:

$$f(n)=g(n)+h(n)$$

   o **g(n)** is the known cost from the start node to n.
   o **h(n)** is the estimated cost from n to the goal (heuristic).

215

o **f(n)** represents the total estimated cost of the cheapest solution through n.

How A Works:*

1. **Initialization:** Start at the initial node and set g(start) = 0 and h(start) to the heuristic estimate of the distance to the goal.
2. **Explore Neighbors:** A* explores the graph by selecting the node with the smallest f(n) value (i.e., the most promising node based on both actual and estimated costs).
3. **Update Costs:** For each neighboring node, calculate the tentative g(n) and f(n) values. If a shorter path to the neighbor is found, update the values.
4. **Repeat:** This process continues until the goal node is reached or all possible paths have been explored.

A Algorithm (Pseudocode):*
scss

```
A* algorithm(graph, start, goal):
    open_list = priority_queue with start node
    closed_list = empty set
    g(start) = 0
    h(start) = heuristic(start, goal)
    f(start) = g(start) + h(start)

    while open_list is not empty:
```

216

```
        current_node = node in open_list with the
lowest f(n)
        if current_node == goal:
            return
reconstruct_path(current_node)

        open_list.remove(current_node)
        closed_list.add(current_node)

        for each neighbor of current_node:
            if neighbor in closed_list:
                continue

            tentative_g  =  g(current_node)  +
cost(current_node, neighbor)
            if  neighbor  not  in  open_list  or
tentative_g < g(neighbor):
                g(neighbor) = tentative_g
                h(neighbor)                    =
heuristic(neighbor, goal)
                f(neighbor)  =  g(neighbor)  +
h(neighbor)
                add neighbor to open_list

    return failure  # No path found
```

How A Differs from Dijkstra's Algorithm*

While **A*** and **Dijkstra's algorithm** are both used for finding the shortest path, they differ in the following ways:

1. Heuristic Function:

- **Dijkstra's algorithm** only considers the **actual cost** ($g(n)$) from the start node to the current node and explores the graph exhaustively.
- **A***, on the other hand, combines the **actual cost** ($g(n)$) and the **heuristic estimate** ($h(n)$) to focus the search toward the goal, thus often exploring fewer nodes and reaching the goal more efficiently.

2. Search Efficiency:

- **Dijkstra's algorithm** is **uninformed** and searches all possible paths equally. It guarantees the shortest path in a graph but can be slower because it doesn't use any knowledge about the goal.
- **A*** is **informed** and uses the heuristic to prioritize exploring nodes that are closer to the goal, which often results in a faster search.

3. Use of Heuristic:

- **Dijkstra's algorithm** doesn't require a heuristic function. It guarantees the shortest path in a graph, regardless of

218

edge weights, as long as the graph doesn't contain negative weights.

- **A*** relies on a **heuristic function** to make informed decisions about which nodes to explore, making it faster but potentially less reliable if the heuristic is not well-designed.

4. Optimality:

- **Dijkstra's algorithm** is always optimal when all edge weights are non-negative.
- **A*** is also optimal, but only if the heuristic function is **admissible** (i.e., it never overestimates the true cost to reach the goal) and **consistent**.

---

*Real-World Applications: A in Games for NPC Pathfinding and AI Simulations**

The **A*** algorithm is used extensively in **games** and **AI simulations** for pathfinding tasks, such as moving Non-Player Characters (NPCs) in games, or planning robot movements in AI simulations. A* is also widely used in **navigation systems** and **autonomous vehicles**.

1. NPC Pathfinding in Games:

In **video games**, NPCs often need to find paths between different locations within a game world, such as moving from one point to another on a map. The A* algorithm is ideal for this task because it efficiently finds the shortest path while considering obstacles and terrain.

- **Example:** In a **strategy game**, an NPC might need to navigate a maze-like environment. A* will allow the NPC to calculate the optimal path from its current position to a target, avoiding obstacles like walls, and using a **heuristic** to guide the search toward the goal.

2. AI Simulations for Robot Movement:

In **robotics**, A* is used for **robot path planning**, where a robot must find the shortest path from its starting point to a destination in an environment with obstacles.

- **Example:** A robot in a **warehouse** needs to navigate through aisles and avoid obstacles like shelves and people. A* can be used to efficiently calculate the best route while factoring in obstacles, walls, and varying terrain.

3. Navigation in GPS Systems:

In **GPS systems**, A* can be used for **route planning** to find the shortest driving or walking route between two locations while considering real-time traffic data and other dynamic factors.

- **Example:** When you search for directions on a GPS app, A* may be used to compute the optimal route from your current location to the destination, considering both distance and traffic conditions. The heuristic could be the straight-line distance or estimated travel time to the goal.

---

*Example: Implementing A Algorithm**

Here is a basic Python implementation of the **A*** algorithm to find the shortest path in a grid, where we consider movement in 4 directions (up, down, left, right):

```python
import heapq

def a_star(grid, start, goal):
    def heuristic(a, b):
        return abs(a[0] - b[0]) + abs(a[1] -
b[1])  # Manhattan distance
```

```
    open_list = []
    heapq.heappush(open_list, (0, start))   #
(f_score, node)
    came_from = {}
    g_score = {start: 0}
    f_score = {start: heuristic(start, goal)}

    while open_list:
        _, current = heapq.heappop(open_list)

        if current == goal:
            # Reconstruct path
            path = []
            while current in came_from:
                path.append(current)
                current = came_from[current]
            path.append(start)
            return path[::-1]  # Reverse path to
start from the beginning

        for neighbor in [(current[0]-1,
current[1]), (current[0]+1, current[1]),
                        (current[0],
current[1]-1), (current[0], current[1]+1)]:
            if 0 <= neighbor[0] < len(grid) and
0 <= neighbor[1] < len(grid[0]) and
grid[neighbor[0]][neighbor[1]] == 0:
                tentative_g_score =
g_score[current] + 1
```

```
            if neighbor not in g_score or
tentative_g_score < g_score[neighbor]:
                came_from[neighbor]          =
current
                g_score[neighbor]            =
tentative_g_score
                f_score[neighbor]            =
g_score[neighbor] + heuristic(neighbor, goal)
                heapq.heappush(open_list,
(f_score[neighbor], neighbor))


    return None   # No path found

# Example grid (0 = free, 1 = obstacle)
grid = [
    [0, 0, 0, 0, 0],
    [0, 1, 1, 0, 0],
    [0, 1, 0, 0, 0],
    [0, 0, 0, 1, 0],
    [0, 0, 0, 0, 0]
]

start = (0, 0)
goal = (4, 4)

path = a_star(grid, start, goal)
print("Path found:", path)
```

Explanation:

- **grid** is a 2D array representing the environment where 0 denotes a free space and 1 denotes an obstacle.
- **a_star** function computes the shortest path from the start to the goal, avoiding obstacles.
- The heuristic used here is the **Manhattan distance**, which is appropriate for grid-based environments.

Output:

pgsql

```
Path found: [(0, 0), (0, 1), (1, 1), (2, 1), (2,
2), (3, 2), (4, 2), (4, 3), (4, 4)]
```

Conclusion

In this chapter, we explored the *A algorithm**, a powerful **pathfinding** algorithm that uses both the **actual cost** and **heuristic estimates** to efficiently find the shortest path between two nodes in a graph. We discussed:

- The **heuristic-driven approach** of A* and how it differs from **Dijkstra's algorithm**.
- The algorithm's **real-world applications** in **games, robot pathfinding**, and **GPS systems**.

- A practical **implementation** of the A* algorithm for pathfinding in a grid-based environment.

A* is widely used for efficient pathfinding in many fields, particularly in scenarios where large and complex graphs need to be navigated. In the next chapter, we will dive into **minimum spanning tree algorithms**, which are used to find the minimum cost to connect all vertices in a graph.

CHAPTER 21

ADVANCED SEARCHING ALGORITHMS: KMP, RABIN-KARP, AND MORE

In the world of computer science, **string matching** is a fundamental problem that arises in many different contexts. Whether it's searching for keywords in a text file, finding substrings in DNA sequences, or identifying patterns in large datasets, efficient string searching is crucial. Traditional string search algorithms like **Naive String Matching** often lead to slow performance, especially when working with large datasets. To address these challenges, **advanced string matching algorithms** like **Knuth-Morris-Pratt (KMP)** and **Rabin-Karp** have been developed, offering significant improvements in search time.

In this chapter, we will:

- Introduce two powerful **advanced string matching algorithms**: **Knuth-Morris-Pratt (KMP)** and **Rabin-Karp**.
- Discuss how these algorithms optimize the search time compared to the naive approach.

- Explore **real-world applications** of these algorithms in **text editors**, **search engines**, and **data mining**.

Introduction to Advanced String Matching Algorithms: KMP and Rabin-Karp

String matching is a process of finding occurrences of a **pattern** (substring) within a **text** (string). The goal is to determine where the pattern appears in the text in the most efficient way possible.

1. Knuth-Morris-Pratt (KMP) Algorithm:

The **Knuth-Morris-Pratt (KMP)** algorithm is an **efficient** string searching algorithm that reduces unnecessary comparisons. It works by preprocessing the pattern (substring) to create a **partial match table** (also known as the **prefix function**), which helps skip redundant comparisons when a mismatch occurs.

How KMP Works:

1. **Preprocessing Phase (Pattern):**
   o Construct a **partial match table** that indicates how much the pattern can be shifted when a mismatch occurs.
   o The table stores the length of the longest prefix that is also a suffix for each prefix of the pattern.

227

2. **Search Phase (Text):**

   o When a mismatch occurs during the comparison between the pattern and the text, the partial match table tells us how much to shift the pattern, avoiding redundant comparisons.

KMP Algorithm (Pseudocode):

```perl
perl
```

```
KMP Search(text, pattern):
    pattern_length = len(pattern)
    text_length = len(text)
    lps = compute_lps(pattern)  # Preprocess the
pattern to create the LPS array

    i = 0  # Pointer for text
    j = 0  # Pointer for pattern

    while i < text_length:
        if pattern[j] == text[i]:
            i += 1
            j += 1

        if j == pattern_length:  # Pattern found
            print("Pattern found at index", i -
j)
            j = lps[j - 1]  # Use LPS to skip
unnecessary comparisons
```

```
        elif i < text_length and pattern[j] !=
text[i]:
            if j != 0:
                j = lps[j - 1]   # Skip the
unnecessary comparisons using LPS
            else:
                i += 1    # Move to the next
character in the text


def compute_lps(pattern):
    lps = [0] * len(pattern)
    length = 0
    i = 1
    while i < len(pattern):
        if pattern[i] == pattern[length]:
            length += 1
            lps[i] = length
            i +- 1
        else:
            if length != 0:
                length = lps[length - 1]
            else:
                lps[i] = 0
                i += 1
    return lps
```

Time Complexity:

- **Preprocessing the pattern (LPS array): O(m)**, where m
  is the length of the pattern.

229

- **Searching the text: O(n)**, where n is the length of the text.

- Overall time complexity: **O(n + m)**, which is much more efficient than the naive approach (O(n * m)).

Key Advantages of KMP:

- **Efficiency:** KMP improves performance by skipping unnecessary comparisons, reducing the time complexity significantly.

- **Optimal for Static Pattern Matching:** Once the preprocessing step is done, KMP can efficiently search for the pattern multiple times in different texts.

---

2. Rabin-Karp Algorithm:

The **Rabin-Karp** algorithm uses a **hashing technique** to find a pattern in a text. It hashes the pattern and the substrings of the text and compares the hashes to quickly locate potential matches. While it may seem slower in the worst case (due to hash collisions), it performs well on average, especially when searching for multiple patterns.

How Rabin-Karp Works:

1. **Preprocessing Phase:**
   o Compute the **hash** value of the pattern.

230

- o Compute the **hash values** of substrings of the text of the same length as the pattern.

2. **Search Phase:**

   - o Compare the hash value of the pattern with the hash value of the current substring of the text.
   - o If the hash values match, a direct comparison of the substring and the pattern is performed to confirm the match.
   - o If the hash values do not match, continue with the next substring.

Rabin-Karp Algorithm (Pseudocode):

python

```
Rabin-Karp Search(text, pattern):
    m = len(pattern)
    n = len(text)
    pattern_hash = hash(pattern)
    current_hash = hash(text[0:m])

    for i = 0 to n - m:
        if current_hash == pattern_hash:
            if text[i:i+m] == pattern:
                print("Pattern found at index",
i)

        if i < n - m:
```

```
        current_hash = rehash(current_hash,
text[i], text[i + m])

def rehash(current_hash, old_char, new_char):
    # Remove old_char's effect and add new_char's
effect on the hash
    current_hash = (current_hash - old_char) *
base + new_char
    return current_hash
```

Time Complexity:

- **Preprocessing (hashing the pattern): O(m)**, where m is the length of the pattern.
- **Searching the text: O(n)** for each substring, but in the worst case, you might have to compare each substring after hashing, which could lead to **O(n * m)** in the worst case with hash collisions.
- Overall time complexity: **O(n + m)** on average, but **O(n * m)** in the worst case.

Key Advantages of Rabin-Karp:

- **Multiple Pattern Matching:** Rabin-Karp is particularly useful for searching for **multiple patterns** in a text simultaneously.
- **Efficient for Large Datasets:** When the pattern length is relatively small, Rabin-Karp performs very efficiently, especially with good hash functions.

Real-World Use Cases: Text Editors, Search Engines, and Data Mining

1. Text Editors:

In text editors (such as **Notepad**, **VS Code**, or **Sublime Text**), searching for keywords or phrases is a common operation. Advanced algorithms like **KMP** and **Rabin-Karp** are used to implement **fast search functions** for locating substrings in large files or documents.

- **KMP** is ideal for single-pattern searches, as it avoids redundant comparisons, speeding up the search process.
- **Rabin-Karp** is useful in cases where **multiple pattern matching** is required, such as searching for a list of keywords in a text.

2. Search Engines:

Search engines, like **Google**, rely on efficient algorithms to match query strings against an enormous corpus of web pages. These algorithms need to perform fast substring searches across millions of web pages.

- **Rabin-Karp** is particularly useful when there are multiple patterns to search for (e.g., keywords or phrases) across large sets of text.
- **KMP** helps optimize the search for a single keyword or phrase, reducing the computation time when matching against a large set of documents.

3. Data Mining:

In **data mining**, pattern matching is used to identify patterns in large datasets, such as identifying frequent sequences in transaction data or detecting anomalies in logs.

- **Rabin-Karp** can be used to quickly find multiple patterns or strings within large datasets.
- **KMP** can be used when looking for specific patterns in data sequences, such as finding matching DNA sequences or identifying repeated patterns in data streams.

Example: Implementing KMP and Rabin-Karp Algorithms

Here's a basic Python implementation of both **KMP** and **Rabin-Karp** algorithms:

```
python
```

```python
# KMP Algorithm Implementation
def kmp_search(text, pattern):
    lps = compute_lps(pattern)
    m, n = len(pattern), len(text)
    i = j = 0

    while i < n:
        if pattern[j] == text[i]:
            i += 1
            j += 1
        if j == m:
            print(f"Pattern found at index {i -
j}")
            j = lps[j - 1]
        elif i < n and pattern[j] != text[i]:
            if j != 0:
                j = lps[j - 1]
            else:
                i += 1

def compute_lps(pattern):
    m = len(pattern)
    lps = [0] * m
    length = 0
    i = 1
    while i < m:
        if pattern[i] == pattern[length]:
            length += 1
```

```
            lps[i] = length
            i += 1
        else:
            if length != 0:
                length = lps[length - 1]
            else:
                lps[i] = 0
                i += 1
    return lps


# Rabin-Karp Algorithm Implementation
def rabin_karp_search(text, pattern):
    m, n = len(pattern), len(text)
    pattern_hash = hash(pattern)
    window_hash = hash(text[:m])

    for i in range(n - m + 1):
        if window_hash == pattern_hash:
            if text[i:i + m] == pattern:
                print(f"Pattern found at index {i}")
        if i < n - m:
            window_hash = hash(text[i+1:i + 1 + m])


# Example usage:
text = "ABABABCABABABCABAB"
pattern = "ABABC"
```

```
print("KMP Search:")
kmp_search(text, pattern)

print("\nRabin-Karp Search:")
rabin_karp_search(text, pattern)
```

Explanation:

- **KMP Search:** We compute the **LPS** array (longest prefix suffix) and use it to avoid redundant comparisons when a mismatch occurs.
- **Rabin-Karp Search:** We calculate the hash of the pattern and compare it with the hash of the text's substrings. If the hashes match, we verify the actual substring.

Conclusion

In this chapter, we explored **advanced string matching algorithms** like **KMP** and **Rabin-Karp**, which optimize search times for pattern matching in strings. These algorithms offer significant improvements over the naive approach by avoiding redundant comparisons and using efficient hashing techniques.

We discussed:

- **KMP's** ability to **optimize search** using a preprocessing step to create a **prefix function**.

- **Rabin-Karp's** reliance on **hashing** to efficiently search for multiple patterns.
- **Real-world applications** in **text editors, search engines,** and **data mining,** where these algorithms play a crucial role in improving search performance.

Both algorithms are essential tools for efficiently solving string matching problems, and their implementation can significantly improve the performance of applications involving large datasets or multiple pattern searches. In the next chapter, we will explore **advanced data structures** for handling complex searching and sorting tasks.

CHAPTER 22

DYNAMIC PROGRAMMING AND GREEDY ALGORITHMS

In problem-solving and algorithm design, two fundamental techniques stand out for optimizing solutions to complex problems: **Dynamic Programming (DP)** and **Greedy Algorithms**. While both techniques aim to find optimal solutions, they differ in their approach to solving problems and the types of problems they are best suited for. Understanding the differences between these strategies and knowing how to apply them can significantly improve your ability to solve a wide range of computational problems efficiently.

In this chapter, we will:

- Examine the **difference between Dynamic Programming (DP)** and **Greedy algorithms**.
- Provide **real-world examples** where DP and greedy algorithms are applied, such as the **Knapsack problem** and **job scheduling**.
- Learn how to approach problems using **DP** and **greedy strategies**.

Difference Between Dynamic Programming (DP) and Greedy Algorithms

1. Dynamic Programming (DP):

Dynamic Programming is an algorithmic technique for solving problems by breaking them down into simpler subproblems and solving each subproblem just once, storing its solution. It is particularly useful for optimization problems, where we want to find the best solution under given constraints.

Key Characteristics of DP:

- **Optimal Substructure:** The problem can be broken down into smaller subproblems that can be solved independently.
- **Overlapping Subproblems:** The subproblems are solved multiple times, so we store their solutions to avoid redundant calculations.
- **Memoization or Tabulation:** In DP, solutions to subproblems are stored in a table (array or matrix) to be reused in the future.

DP Approach:

- Start with the base case(s) and build up the solution by solving smaller subproblems.

- Store the results of the subproblems in a table (either top-down with memoization or bottom-up with tabulation).
- Use these stored results to build the final solution.

2. Greedy Algorithms:

A **Greedy algorithm** makes the locally optimal choice at each step, with the hope that these local solutions will lead to a globally optimal solution. Unlike DP, greedy algorithms do not consider previously computed solutions but rather make decisions based on the current state.

Key Characteristics of Greedy Algorithms:

- **Greedy Choice Property:** A global optimum can be arrived at by selecting a local optimum.
- **No Backtracking:** Once a decision is made, it is never revisited. Greedy algorithms don't reconsider their choices.
- **Used for Optimization Problems:** Typically used when the problem has the **greedy-choice property**, where local optimization leads to global optimization.

Greedy Approach:

- Choose the best option available at each step.
- Make the decision based on current information without worrying about past or future steps.

241

- Continue until a complete solution is found.

Real-World Examples: DP for Knapsack Problem, Greedy Algorithms for Job Scheduling

1. Dynamic Programming: The Knapsack Problem

The **Knapsack problem** is a classic optimization problem where you are given a set of items, each with a weight and a value, and you need to determine the most valuable combination of items that fit within a given weight limit.

Problem Description:

- **Given:** A set of n items, each with a weight w_i and value v_i, and a knapsack with a weight capacity W.
- **Goal:** Find the maximum value of items that can be included in the knapsack without exceeding the weight capacity W.

Dynamic Programming Approach to Knapsack:

- **State:** Let `dp[i][w]` represent the maximum value that can be obtained by considering the first i items and a knapsack capacity of w.
- **Recurrence Relation:**

242

$$dp[i][w] = \max(dp[i-1][w], dp[i-1][w-wi]+vi) \text{ if } wi \leq wd$$

p[i][w] = \max(dp[i-1][w], dp[i-1][w-wi] + vi) \quad \text{if } } wi \leq

$$wdp[i][w] = \max(dp[i-1][w], dp[i-1][w-wi]+vi) \text{ if } wi \leq w$$

- o The first term represents not taking the current item.
- o The second term represents taking the current item and adding its value to the maximum value of the remaining capacity.

Knapsack Algorithm (Pseudocode):

sql

```
Knapsack(weights, values, W, n):
    Create dp table of size (n+1) x (W+1)
    for i = 0 to n:
        for w = 0 to W:
            if i == 0 or w == 0:
                dp[i][w] = 0
            else if weights[i-1] <= w:
                dp[i][w] = max(dp[i-1][w], dp[i-
1][w-weights[i-1]] + values[i-1])
            else:
                dp[i][w] = dp[i-1][w]
    return dp[n][W]
```

Time Complexity:

- **O(n * W)**, where n is the number of items and W is the capacity of the knapsack. This is because we fill an n x W matrix.

Space Complexity:

- **O(n * W)**, for storing the DP table.

The **Knapsack problem** is a classic example of using dynamic programming to solve an optimization problem where decisions depend on previous solutions.

2. Greedy Algorithm: Job Scheduling Problem

The **Job Scheduling problem** is a classic greedy problem where you are given a set of jobs, each with a start time, finish time, and profit, and the goal is to select the maximum profit subset of jobs that don't overlap.

Problem Description:

- **Given:** A set of jobs where each job i has a start time si, finish time fi, and profit pi.
- **Goal:** Select the maximum profit subset of jobs such that no two selected jobs overlap in time.

244

Greedy Approach:

1. Sort jobs by their **finish times**.
2. Start with the first job, and then select the next job that doesn't overlap with the already selected jobs.
3. Repeat the process until no more jobs can be selected.

Job Scheduling Algorithm (Pseudocode):

sql

```
JobScheduling(jobs):
    Sort jobs by finish time
    result = []
    last_finish_time = -1

    for each job in jobs:
        if job.start_time >= last_finish_time:
            result.append(job)
            last_finish_time = job.finish_time

    return result
```

Time Complexity:

- Sorting jobs takes **O(n log n)**, where n is the number of jobs. The greedy selection takes **O(n)**, so the overall time complexity is **O(n log n)**.

Space Complexity:

- **O(n)**, for storing the selected jobs.

The **Job Scheduling problem** is a typical example of a greedy algorithm where the locally optimal choice (selecting the job with the earliest finish time) leads to a globally optimal solution.

How to Approach Problems Using DP and Greedy Strategies

When to Use Dynamic Programming:

1. **Optimal Substructure:** If a problem can be broken down into smaller subproblems whose solutions can be combined to form the solution to the original problem.
2. **Overlapping Subproblems:** If the problem involves subproblems that repeat multiple times (e.g., in the Knapsack problem, the same subproblems are solved multiple times).
3. **Examples:**
   - **Knapsack problem**
   - **Longest common subsequence**
   - **Matrix chain multiplication**
   - **Fibonacci sequence**

When to Use Greedy Algorithms:

1. **Greedy Choice Property:** If a problem can be solved by making a series of locally optimal choices that lead to a globally optimal solution.

2. **No Backtracking:** Greedy algorithms do not reconsider their choices once they are made.

3. **Examples:**
   - **Job scheduling**
   - **Activity selection**
   - **Huffman coding**
   - **Minimum spanning trees (Prim's and Kruskal's)**

General Approach to Choosing Between DP and Greedy Algorithms:

- **Check for overlapping subproblems and optimal substructure:** If the problem involves overlapping subproblems and optimal substructure, DP is typically a better choice.

- **Check for greedy choice property:** If a problem allows for making greedy choices at each step that lead to an optimal solution, a greedy algorithm may be more efficient.

- **Solution Verification:** After solving the problem, verify if the greedy algorithm always provides an optimal solution. If not, DP may be necessary.

Conclusion

In this chapter, we examined **Dynamic Programming (DP) and Greedy algorithms**, two powerful techniques for solving optimization problems. We:

- Differentiated between DP and Greedy approaches, highlighting their respective strengths and weaknesses.
- Provided real-world examples, such as the **Knapsack problem** (DP) and **Job Scheduling** (Greedy).
- Discussed how to approach problems by determining whether DP or Greedy is appropriate based on the problem's characteristics.

Both DP and Greedy algorithms play an essential role in solving complex optimization problems, and understanding when to apply each can lead to more efficient solutions. In the next chapter, we will delve into **graph algorithms**, including **shortest path** and **minimum spanning tree** algorithms.

CHAPTER 23

ADVANCED TECHNIQUES IN SORTING: MERGE SORT, QUICK SORT, AND BEYOND

Sorting is one of the most fundamental operations in computer science. The importance of sorting algorithms lies in their widespread application in **searching**, **data organization**, and **optimization**. While simple algorithms like **Bubble Sort** and **Insertion Sort** have their uses, they are inefficient for large datasets. This chapter will focus on more advanced sorting algorithms like **Merge Sort** and **Quick Sort**, and we will also introduce other advanced algorithms such as **Radix Sort, Bucket Sort**, and **Counting Sort**, which offer even better performance in specific contexts.

In this chapter, we will:

- Review **Merge Sort** and **Quick Sort**, two of the most commonly used divide-and-conquer sorting algorithms.
- Explore **Radix Sort, Bucket Sort**, and **Counting Sort**, which are non-comparative sorting algorithms designed for specialized scenarios.

- Discuss the **use cases** of these algorithms in **high-performance applications** and **sorting large datasets**.

Reviewing Advanced Sorting Algorithms: Merge Sort and Quick Sort

1. Merge Sort

Merge Sort is a **divide-and-conquer** algorithm that recursively divides the array into two halves, sorts each half, and then merges the sorted halves. It is known for its stable performance and is widely used in situations where stability is important (i.e., elements with equal values maintain their relative order).

How Merge Sort Works:

1. **Divide**: Recursively divide the array into two halves until each subarray has only one element.
2. **Conquer**: Sort each of the two halves. Since the array is divided into single elements, the sorting step is trivial.
3. **Combine**: Merge the two sorted halves into a single sorted array.

Merge Sort Algorithm (Pseudocode):

python

```
MergeSort(arr):
    if len(arr) > 1:
        mid = len(arr) // 2  # Find the middle of
the array
        left_half = arr[:mid]
        right_half = arr[mid:]

        MergeSort(left_half)  # Recursively sort
the first half
        MergeSort(right_half)     #   Recursively
sort the second half

        i = j = k = 0
        # Merge the sorted halves
        while  i  <  len(left_half)  and  j  <
len(right_half):
            if left_half[i] < right_half[j]:
                arr[k] = left_half[i]
                i += 1
            else:
                arr[k] = right_half[j]
                j += 1
            k += 1

        # If any elements remain in left_half or
right_half
        while i < len(left_half):
            arr[k] = left_half[i]
            i += 1
```

```
        k += 1
    while j < len(right_half):
        arr[k] = right_half[j]
        j += 1
        k += 1
```

Time Complexity:

- **Best, Average, and Worst Case: O(n log n)**, where n is the number of elements in the array. The merging step takes linear time, and the recursion depth is logarithmic.

Space Complexity:

- **O(n)**, as additional space is needed for the temporary subarrays during the merging process.

Merge Sort is particularly useful for sorting **linked lists** and is also effective for sorting **large datasets** that don't fit entirely in memory (due to its external sorting capabilities).

---

2. Quick Sort

Quick Sort is another **divide-and-conquer** sorting algorithm, but unlike **Merge Sort**, it uses a **partitioning** approach. It picks an element as a **pivot** and partitions the array around the pivot such that elements less than the pivot come before it, and elements greater than the pivot come after it. The subarrays are then recursively sorted.

How Quick Sort Works:

1. **Choose a Pivot:** Select a pivot element from the array (various strategies for selecting the pivot, such as first element, last element, or median).
2. **Partitioning:** Rearrange the array so that all elements less than the pivot are on the left, and all elements greater than the pivot are on the right.
3. **Recursion:** Recursively apply the same process to the left and right subarrays.

Quick Sort Algorithm (Pseudocode):

scss

```
QuickSort(arr, low, high):
    if low < high:
        pivot_index = Partition(arr, low, high)
        QuickSort(arr, low, pivot_index - 1)
        QuickSort(arr, pivot_index + 1, high)


Partition(arr, low, high):
    pivot = arr[high]   # Choose the last element
as the pivot
    i = low - 1
    for j = low to high - 1:
```

```
    if arr[j] <= pivot:
        i += 1
        swap arr[i] with arr[j]
    swap arr[i + 1] with arr[high]
    return i + 1
```

Time Complexity:

- **Best and Average Case: O(n log n)**, when the pivot splits the array evenly.
- **Worst Case: O(n²)**, when the pivot is the smallest or largest element, leading to unbalanced partitions. However, with random pivot selection or the median of three technique, the worst-case performance can be avoided.

Space Complexity:

- **O(log n)** for the recursive stack in the average case, but in the worst case, it can go up to **O(n)**.

Quick Sort is preferred for **in-memory sorting** due to its **average-case efficiency** and lower space complexity compared to Merge Sort. However, in cases where **worst-case performance** is critical, it may not be suitable without precautions like randomized pivot selection.

Introduction to More Advanced Sorting Algorithms: Radix Sort, Bucket Sort, Counting Sort

In addition to **Merge Sort** and **Quick Sort**, there are several other advanced sorting algorithms that are particularly effective in specific contexts, such as when the input data is limited to a specific range or when elements can be processed in **linear time**.

1. Radix Sort

Radix Sort is a non-comparative sorting algorithm that works by sorting the elements digit by digit, starting from the least significant digit. It uses **counting sort** as a subroutine to sort the digits.

How Radix Sort Works:

1. **Sort by Least Significant Digit:** Start by sorting the elements based on the least significant digit (e.g., units place).
2. **Move to Next Digit:** Once the least significant digit is sorted, move to the next more significant digit and repeat the process.
3. **Repeat:** Continue this process until all digits have been processed.

Time Complexity:

- **O(nk)**, where n is the number of elements and k is the number of digits in the largest number. When k is small (i.e., the number of digits is small relative to the number of elements), Radix Sort performs very efficiently.

Space Complexity:

- **O(n)**, for storing the counting sort array.

Radix Sort is particularly effective when sorting **integers** or **fixed-length strings**.

---

2. Bucket Sort

Bucket Sort divides the elements into a number of **buckets**, each representing a range of values. Each bucket is then sorted individually (often using a different sorting algorithm), and the contents of the buckets are concatenated to produce the final sorted list.

How Bucket Sort Works:

1. **Divide into Buckets:** Divide the range of the dataset into equally spaced buckets.

2. **Distribute Elements into Buckets:** Place each element into the corresponding bucket based on its value.

3. **Sort Individual Buckets:** Sort the individual buckets (using any sorting algorithm, often **Insertion Sort**).

4. **Concatenate Buckets:** Combine the sorted buckets into the final sorted array.

Time Complexity:

- **O(n + k)**, where n is the number of elements and k is the number of buckets. If the data is uniformly distributed, the sorting step within each bucket is relatively fast.

Space Complexity:

- **O(n + k)**, for the buckets and the temporary storage.

Bucket Sort is effective when the data is **uniformly distributed** and works best for **floating-point numbers** or **range-limited integers**.

---

3. Counting Sort

Counting Sort is an integer sorting algorithm that works by counting the occurrences of each distinct element in the array. It is not a comparison-based algorithm, making it efficient for sorting integers within a known range.

257

How Counting Sort Works:

1. **Count Occurrences:** Count how many times each element appears in the input array.
2. **Compute Cumulative Count:** Compute the cumulative count of elements to determine their final position in the sorted array.
3. **Place Elements in Sorted Order:** Place each element in its correct position in the sorted output array.

Time Complexity:

- **O(n + k)**, where n is the number of elements and k is the range of the input data.

Space Complexity:

- **O(k)**, for storing the count array.

Counting Sort is ideal for **sorting integers** when the range of numbers is not significantly larger than the number of elements in the array.

Use Cases in High-Performance Applications and Sorting Large Datasets

1. Sorting Large Datasets:

In **big data applications**, sorting large datasets efficiently is crucial. Algorithms like **Radix Sort**, **Bucket Sort**, and **Counting Sort** are useful when the input is constrained to a limited range or when the data is not comparable in the traditional sense (such as strings or floating-point numbers).

2. Parallel Sorting:

Algorithms like **Merge Sort** can be parallelized to improve performance when sorting large datasets. In **multi-threaded** or **distributed systems**, sorting can be done in parallel to divide and conquer the workload.

3. Memory-Constrained Environments:

For environments with limited memory, algorithms like **Quick Sort** and **Merge Sort** (which have lower space complexity than others like **Radix Sort**) are useful. In contrast, **Counting Sort** and **Bucket Sort** may require more memory but perform faster for specific datasets.

Conclusion

In this chapter, we explored **advanced sorting algorithms** like **Merge Sort**, **Quick Sort**, **Radix Sort**, **Bucket Sort**, and **Counting Sort**. These algorithms offer a variety of advantages depending on the type of data and the problem context. We:

- Reviewed the **divide-and-conquer** nature of **Merge Sort** and **Quick Sort**, highlighting their strengths and weaknesses.
- Introduced non-comparative algorithms like **Radix Sort**, **Bucket Sort**, and **Counting Sort**, which excel in specific scenarios, such as sorting large datasets or numbers in a known range.
- Discussed their **real-world use cases**, including high-performance applications, sorting in distributed systems, and working with large or complex datasets.

Choosing the right sorting algorithm can significantly affect the performance of your application, especially when working with large datasets. In the next chapter, we will dive into **advanced graph algorithms**, including **minimum spanning tree** and **shortest path** algorithms.

CHAPTER 24

COMPUTATIONAL GEOMETRY: ALGORITHMS FOR GEOMETRIC PROBLEMS

Computational Geometry is a field of computer science that deals with the design and analysis of algorithms for solving geometric problems. These problems arise in various fields such as computer graphics, robotics, geographic information systems (GIS), and CAD (Computer-Aided Design). In essence, computational geometry focuses on the efficient processing and manipulation of geometric data.

In this chapter, we will:

- Discuss the **basics of computational geometry** and how algorithms handle geometric data.
- Introduce **common geometric algorithms** like the **convex hull, closest pair of points**, and **line intersection**.
- Explore **real-world applications** of computational geometry in **Geographic Information Systems (GIS)** and **computer graphics**.

Basics of Computational Geometry and How Algorithms Deal with Geometric Data

At the core of computational geometry is the concept of geometric objects, such as points, lines, polygons, and more complex shapes. The challenge is to develop efficient algorithms for processing these objects to solve specific problems.

Geometric Objects:

- **Points**: A point is a fundamental object, usually represented by a pair of coordinates (x, y).
- **Lines**: A line in 2D space can be defined by two points, or in other forms like slope-intercept form (y = mx + b).
- **Polygons**: Polygons are closed shapes made up of a sequence of line segments. Examples include triangles, rectangles, and more complex shapes.

Geometric Problems:

- Many geometric problems involve **comparing, sorting,** and **partitioning** geometric objects. For example, determining whether two line segments **intersect** or finding the **closest pair of points** in a dataset.

Algorithmic Approach:

- **Divide and conquer**: Some geometric algorithms, like **convex hull** algorithms, use divide-and-conquer strategies to solve problems by breaking them down into simpler subproblems.
- **Sweep line**: This technique involves moving a conceptual line across the plane and solving problems at each step.
- **Data structures**: Efficient geometric algorithms often rely on specialized data structures like **segment trees, k-d trees**, and **balanced binary search trees** to store and query geometric data efficiently.

Common Geometric Algorithms

1. Convex Hull Algorithm

The **convex hull** of a set of points is the smallest convex polygon that encloses all the points. In other words, it's the "tightest" boundary that contains all the points. This is useful in problems like **collision detection, shape recognition**, and **map outlining**.

How the Convex Hull Algorithm Works:

1. **Graham's Scan** or **Jarvis's March** are two popular algorithms for computing the convex hull. Both

algorithms work by sorting the points and iteratively finding the vertices that form the convex boundary.

2. The algorithm starts by sorting the points, then uses a **stack** to keep track of the boundary points.

Graham's Scan Algorithm (Pseudocode):

arduino

```
ConvexHull(points):
    Sort points by polar angle with respect to
the leftmost point
    Create an empty stack
    Push the first three points onto the stack
    For each remaining point:
        while stack has more than 1 point and
angle between stack[-2], stack[-1], and
current_point is not counter-clockwise:
            pop the top of the stack
        push the current point onto the stack
    return the points in the stack
```

Time Complexity:

- Sorting the points takes **O(n log n)**.
- The convex hull construction step takes **O(n)**.
- Overall time complexity: **O(n log n)**.

2. Closest Pair of Points Algorithm

The **closest pair of points** problem is to find the two points in a given set of points that are closest to each other. This problem has applications in **image processing**, **cluster analysis**, and **robotics**.

How the Closest Pair of Points Algorithm Works:

- **Divide and conquer**: The algorithm divides the points into two halves and recursively computes the closest pair in each half. Then, it checks if the closest pair across the two halves is closer than the pairs found in the individual halves.
- The key to efficiency is in sorting the points and using **merge** to check possible pairs across the dividing line.

Closest Pair of Points Algorithm (Pseudocode):

sql

```
ClosestPair(points):
    Sort the points by x-coordinate
    Divide the points into two halves
    Recursively find the closest pair in the left
and right halves
    Check for possible closer pairs across the
boundary
    Return the minimum distance
```

Time Complexity:

- Sorting the points: **O(n log n)**.
- The divide and conquer step takes **O(n log n)**.

Overall time complexity: **O(n log n)**.

---

3. Line Intersection Algorithm

The **line intersection** problem involves determining whether two line segments intersect. This problem is fundamental in **computer graphics**, **robotics**, and **geometric modeling**.

How the Line Intersection Algorithm Works:

- The algorithm sorts the line segments by their **x-coordinates** and then uses a **sweep line** technique to check for intersections as the line "sweeps" across the plane.
- A data structure like a **balanced binary search tree** is often used to maintain the status of the line segments that intersect the sweep line at a given moment.

Line Intersection Algorithm (Pseudocode):

```sql
LineIntersection(segments):
```

```
Sort the line segments by their starting
point (x-coordinate)
Initialize a balanced binary search tree
(BST)
For each segment:
Check for intersection with segments
currently in the BST
Add or remove segments from the BST as
the sweep line moves
Return all intersections
```

Time Complexity:

- Sorting the segments takes **O(n log n)**.
- The sweep line algorithm, with efficient handling of segment events, operates in **O(n log n)**.
- Overall time complexity: **O(n log n)**.

Real-World Applications in GIS and Computer Graphics

1. Geographic Information Systems (GIS):

In **GIS**, computational geometry plays a critical role in analyzing spatial data. Algorithms like the **convex hull** are used to identify the boundary of geographic features (e.g., city boundaries), and

closest pair of points algorithms are used to find the nearest locations (e.g., finding the closest hospital or gas station).

- **Convex Hull:** GIS systems often need to compute the boundary of a region, which can be represented by the convex hull of a set of points (e.g., landmarks or geographic coordinates).
- **Closest Pair of Points:** In **route optimization** or **location analysis**, the closest pair algorithm helps find the nearest facilities or services to a given location.
- **Line Intersection:** Used in **network analysis** to detect and resolve overlapping or intersecting roads, utilities, or pipelines.

2. Computer Graphics:

In **computer graphics**, computational geometry is used to model and render 2D and 3D objects efficiently. For example, algorithms like the **convex hull** are used in **collision detection,** where the convex hull helps simplify the shape of objects, making collision detection faster.

- **Convex Hull:** Used to model **collision boundaries** in simulations or video games, where the convex hull represents the simplest boundary for detecting potential collisions between objects.

- **Closest Pair of Points:** In graphics, this algorithm can help with **rendering** tasks, such as finding the nearest light source to an object in a scene for shading calculations.

- **Line Intersection:** Essential in **ray tracing** and **visibility calculations**, where intersections of rays with surfaces or objects need to be detected.

3. Robotics and Motion Planning:

In **robotics**, algorithms in computational geometry are crucial for tasks such as **motion planning, obstacle avoidance**, and **pathfinding**. The **convex hull** algorithm helps identify free spaces, and the **line intersection** algorithm is used to check if obstacles block a robot's path.

- **Convex Hull:** Used for **collision-free motion planning**, where robots avoid obstacles represented as polygons.

- **Line Intersection:** Used for checking if a robot's movement path intersects with any obstacles.

Conclusion

In this chapter, we introduced **computational geometry** and its critical role in solving geometric problems. We explored:

- **Common geometric algorithms**, including **convex hull**, **closest pair of points**, and **line intersection**, which solve fundamental problems in geometry.
- **Real-world applications** in fields such as **GIS**, **computer graphics**, and **robotics**, where computational geometry is used to analyze and manipulate geometric data.

As computational problems become more complex, the need for efficient geometric algorithms grows, and computational geometry continues to be a fundamental area in the development of algorithms for real-world applications. In the next chapter, we will delve into **advanced graph algorithms** for optimizing network flow and connectivity problems.

CHAPTER 25

PARALLEL ALGORITHMS: MAXIMIZING PERFORMANCE IN MULTI-CORE SYSTEMS

With the rise of multi-core processors in modern computing systems, parallel computing has become a key technique to significantly enhance performance. Parallel algorithms enable the simultaneous execution of multiple tasks, allowing computationally expensive operations to be performed more quickly. In this chapter, we will explore the concepts of **parallel computing** and **parallel algorithms**, focusing on how they are used to maximize performance on **multi-core systems**.

In this chapter, we will:

- Introduce **parallel computing** and discuss its advantages over traditional serial computing.
- Explain how to **split tasks efficiently** to leverage multiple processor cores.
- Provide **real-world examples** of **parallel sorting algorithms** and **matrix multiplication**, two common tasks that benefit greatly from parallelization.

271

Introduction to Parallel Computing and Parallel Algorithms

What is Parallel Computing?

Parallel computing is a type of computation where tasks are divided into smaller sub-tasks that can be processed simultaneously across multiple processors (or cores). In a parallel system, multiple processors or cores work together on different parts of a problem to complete the task faster.

In contrast to **serial computing**, where tasks are executed one after another on a single processor, **parallel computing** can drastically reduce the time it takes to process large datasets, perform complex calculations, or execute time-sensitive applications.

Parallel Algorithms:

A **parallel algorithm** is an algorithm designed to take advantage of multiple processors by breaking down a problem into smaller subproblems that can be solved concurrently. The efficiency of a parallel algorithm depends on how well the problem is decomposed and how tasks are distributed across processors.

Key principles for designing efficient parallel algorithms:

- **Task Decomposition:** The problem is broken into smaller, independent subproblems.

- **Data Distribution:** Data is partitioned or distributed across multiple processors.

- **Synchronization:** Proper management of data dependencies and coordination between processors to ensure correct results.

- **Load Balancing:** Ensuring that each processor has an approximately equal amount of work to do to avoid bottlenecks.

How to Split Tasks Efficiently to Run on Multiple Cores

The performance of parallel algorithms largely depends on how tasks are divided and distributed across the available cores. The key challenge is finding the right balance between splitting tasks into manageable subproblems and avoiding excessive overhead from coordination or communication between cores.

Task Decomposition and Parallelization Strategies:

1. **Divide-and-Conquer:** A problem is recursively divided into smaller subproblems until they are simple enough to be solved independently. This strategy works well for

273

many parallel algorithms, such as **sorting** and **matrix multiplication**.

2. **Data Parallelism:** The problem is decomposed by distributing data across processors. Each processor performs the same operation on different pieces of data simultaneously. This is common in tasks like **vector processing** or **image manipulation**.

3. **Pipeline Parallelism:** Tasks are divided into stages, and each stage is executed on a different core. This is often used in streaming applications, where data is processed in a sequence of operations.

4. **Task Parallelism:** Independent tasks are assigned to different processors, which can execute concurrently. This approach is useful when tasks are heterogeneous and do not rely on a specific order of execution.

Synchronization and Communication:

- When tasks are split into subproblems, some synchronization may be necessary to ensure that all processors coordinate properly and produce the correct final result. This could involve **barriers, locks,** or **message passing** between processors.

- **Data sharing** or **communication** overhead can affect performance if processors frequently need to exchange information. Algorithms should minimize these interactions to maximize efficiency.

Example: Parallel Sorting Algorithms

Sorting is one of the most common tasks in computing, and there are many sorting algorithms that can be parallelized to improve performance. Here, we will look at two well-known parallel sorting algorithms: **Merge Sort** and **Quick Sort**.

1. Parallel Merge Sort

Merge Sort is a divide-and-conquer algorithm that splits the array into two halves, sorts them recursively, and then merges them. Parallelizing **Merge Sort** involves splitting the array and sorting each half concurrently.

How Parallel Merge Sort Works:

1. **Divide:** Split the array into two halves.
2. **Sort:** Sort the two halves in parallel using **Merge Sort**.
3. **Merge:** Merge the two sorted halves into a single sorted array.

This can be efficiently parallelized by using multiple threads to sort the two halves of the array. The merging process can also be parallelized by dividing the merging of two sorted subarrays into smaller chunks.

Time Complexity:

- **Serial Merge Sort:** O(n log n)
- **Parallel Merge Sort:** The time complexity remains **O(n log n)**, but the constants involved are reduced due to parallelism. If there are p processors, the depth of recursion can be reduced, making the sorting process faster.

2. Parallel Quick Sort

Quick Sort is another divide-and-conquer algorithm that uses a pivot to partition the array into two subarrays. In the parallel version of Quick Sort, the left and right partitions are sorted concurrently.

How Parallel Quick Sort Works:

1. **Pivot Selection:** Choose a pivot element.
2. **Partitioning:** Partition the array into two subarrays such that elements less than the pivot are on the left and elements greater than the pivot are on the right.
3. **Sort:** Recursively sort the two subarrays in parallel.

Since the partitioning step is done independently for each subarray, the recursive sorting can be done in parallel on different processors.

276

Time Complexity:

- **Serial Quick Sort:** O(n log n) on average, but it can degrade to O(n²) in the worst case.
- **Parallel Quick Sort:** The average case time complexity remains **O(n log n)**, with improved constants in the parallel case, particularly when the depth of the recursion is reduced.

Example: Parallel Matrix Multiplication

Matrix multiplication is another computationally intensive task that benefits from parallelization, particularly when working with large matrices. In matrix multiplication, we multiply two matrices A (of size m x n) and B (of size n x p) to produce a matrix C (of size m x p), where each element in matrix C is the dot product of a row of A and a column of B.

How Parallel Matrix Multiplication Works:

1. **Divide the Work:** Each row of matrix A can be multiplied with each column of matrix B independently to produce the corresponding element of matrix C. This allows for parallel processing of the individual elements of C.

277

2. **Parallelize the Dot Product:** Each dot product (i.e., the multiplication and summation of corresponding elements from a row and column) can be computed in parallel across multiple processors.

Time Complexity:

- **Serial Matrix Multiplication:** O(m * n * p)
- **Parallel Matrix Multiplication:** If there are p processors, the overall time complexity is reduced by distributing the computation of each element across multiple processors. The time complexity remains **O(m * n * p)**, but the execution time is reduced by splitting the tasks.

Real-World Applications of Parallel Algorithms

1. High-Performance Computing (HPC):

In HPC systems, parallel algorithms are used extensively to solve problems that involve massive datasets or complex computations, such as **scientific simulations**, **weather forecasting**, and **molecular modeling**. These tasks are often parallelized to take advantage of multi-core processors or distributed systems, enabling faster and more efficient computation.

2. Data Processing and Analytics:

Large-scale data processing tasks, such as sorting, searching, and analyzing big data, can be parallelized to improve performance. For example:

- **MapReduce** frameworks, like **Hadoop** and **Spark**, parallelize the processing of large datasets across clusters of machines. Tasks like sorting or aggregating data are distributed across nodes for faster computation.

3. Video Rendering and Computer Graphics:

Parallel algorithms are also applied in **computer graphics** for rendering 3D images or performing complex image transformations. Tasks such as ray tracing, image processing, and rendering in video games benefit from parallel computing, especially with the advent of **GPUs** (Graphics Processing Units), which are optimized for parallel tasks.

4. Machine Learning:

In **machine learning**, training large models with vast amounts of data can be accelerated using parallel algorithms. For example, **training deep neural networks** or performing **matrix operations** during model optimization can be parallelized to take advantage of multi-core systems or GPUs.

Conclusion

In this chapter, we explored **parallel algorithms** and how they maximize performance in **multi-core systems**. We discussed:

- The **basics of parallel computing**, including the importance of splitting tasks efficiently and distributing them across multiple processors.
- **Examples of parallel algorithms** for common tasks like **sorting** and **matrix multiplication**.
- **Real-world applications** of parallel algorithms in fields such as **high-performance computing, data analytics, machine learning**, and **computer graphics**.

Parallel computing plays a vital role in speeding up the processing of large datasets and complex tasks, and understanding how to design and implement parallel algorithms is essential for optimizing modern applications. In the next chapter, we will dive into **distributed algorithms** and explore how they can be used in large-scale, distributed systems for tasks like data consistency and fault tolerance.

CHAPTER 26

DISTRIBUTED DATA STRUCTURES: BUILDING RESILIENT AND SCALABLE SYSTEMS

In today's world, where systems must handle vast amounts of data and scale effectively, the need for **distributed data structures** has become paramount. **Distributed data structures** are a set of techniques that allow data to be stored, accessed, and modified across multiple machines in a network. These data structures are designed to ensure **resilience, scalability,** and **availability** in distributed systems.

In this chapter, we will:

- Explore the **concepts of distributed data structures** and understand their role in distributed systems.
- Dive into specific techniques such as **consistent hashing, distributed hash tables (DHTs),** and **quorum-based approaches**.

- Examine real-world applications of distributed data structures in **distributed storage systems** like **Amazon DynamoDB** and **Google Bigtable**.

Concepts of Distributed Data Structures and Their Role in Distributed Systems

What are Distributed Data Structures?

A **distributed data structure** is a data structure that is designed to work across multiple nodes in a distributed system, where the nodes may be geographically separated or may experience failures. These data structures are the building blocks of systems that need to scale horizontally, providing both **availability** and **resilience**.

The key challenges for distributed data structures include:

1. **Fault Tolerance**: Ensuring that the system remains operational even when some nodes fail.
2. **Scalability**: Ensuring the system can grow by adding more nodes without affecting performance.
3. **Consistency**: Maintaining data consistency across nodes, especially in the presence of network partitions or failures.

Distributed systems use a variety of techniques to address these challenges, including **replication, partitioning**, and **distributed algorithms**.

Role in Distributed Systems:

Distributed data structures are fundamental to the success of distributed systems because they allow the system to:

- **Distribute data** across multiple nodes or machines for load balancing.
- **Replicate data** to ensure high availability, even if some nodes fail.
- **Maintain consistency** through synchronization mechanisms, ensuring that updates to data are reflected across all nodes in a predictable manner.

Key Techniques in Distributed Data Structures

1. Consistent Hashing

Consistent hashing is a technique used to distribute data across a **ring** of nodes in a way that minimizes the number of data migrations when nodes are added or removed. This approach is widely used in systems that need to scale horizontally, such as **distributed caches** or **key-value stores**.

283

How Consistent Hashing Works:

1. **Hashing Nodes**: Nodes are hashed to positions on a ring (using a hash function). Each node is assigned a position on the ring, and the data is distributed according to the hash of its key.

2. **Key Assignment**: Data keys are also hashed and placed on the ring. A key will be stored on the node that is closest to it in the clockwise direction.

3. **Adding/Removing Nodes**: When a new node is added, only the keys that hash to the new node's position will need to be redistributed. This minimizes the impact of node additions and removals, unlike traditional hashing approaches.

Advantages:

- Reduces the need for **rebalancing** when nodes are added or removed.
- **Scalable**: As the number of nodes increases, consistent hashing ensures that only a small portion of keys need to be redistributed.

Real-World Example:

In **distributed caches** (like **Memcached**), consistent hashing is used to assign keys to servers in a way that minimizes the number of keys that need to be moved when the cache is scaled.

2. Distributed Hash Tables (DHTs)

A **Distributed Hash Table (DHT)** is a distributed system that provides a hash table-like interface, where keys are mapped to values across multiple nodes in the system. Each node in a DHT is responsible for a portion of the key-space, and the DHT ensures that data can be retrieved efficiently from any node.

How DHTs Work:

- **Key Distribution**: DHTs use consistent hashing (or similar techniques) to map data keys to nodes. Each node in the DHT is responsible for storing a set of keys.
- **Node Lookup**: When a client needs to retrieve data associated with a key, the system uses the hash function to determine which node is responsible for that key and queries that node directly.
- **Replication**: DHTs often replicate data across multiple nodes for fault tolerance.

Popular DHT Implementations:

- **Chord**: A DHT algorithm that organizes nodes in a ring and allows efficient lookups for data.
- **Kademlia**: A more recent DHT design that uses a XOR-based distance metric to efficiently route queries.

285

Advantages of DHTs:

- **Scalable**: DHTs scale well as the number of nodes increases.
- **Fault-Tolerant**: DHTs are resilient to node failures through replication and decentralization.
- **Efficient**: DHTs allow for efficient lookups with logarithmic time complexity, even in large systems.

Real-World Example:

BitTorrent uses a DHT (specifically, the **Kademlia DHT**) to track the locations of files across a distributed network. Each peer stores information about parts of files and can retrieve or serve pieces of files to others efficiently.

---

3. Quorum-Based Approaches

Quorum-based approaches are used to ensure consistency in distributed systems, especially when data is replicated across multiple nodes. A **quorum** is the minimum number of nodes that need to participate in a read or write operation to ensure that the operation is successful and the data remains consistent.

How Quorum-Based Approaches Work:

1. **Quorum for Writes**: For a write operation to be considered successful, it must be acknowledged by a certain number of nodes, known as the **write quorum**.

2. **Quorum for Reads**: Similarly, for a read operation to return valid data, it must be fetched from a certain number of nodes, known as the **read quorum**.

3. **Conflict Resolution**: If there are inconsistencies between replicas (due to different nodes being updated at different times), the system uses conflict resolution techniques to reconcile the differences.

Example:

- In systems like **Amazon DynamoDB**, a **read quorum** and **write quorum** are used to ensure consistency across nodes while maintaining availability, especially in cases of network partitions or failures.

Advantages:

- **Consistency and Availability**: Quorum-based approaches provide a good balance between **availability** and **consistency**, as nodes can still respond to requests even if not all replicas are available.

- **Fault-Tolerant**: They ensure that operations can still be carried out even in the face of some node failures.

Real-World Applications: Distributed Storage Systems

1. Amazon DynamoDB

Amazon DynamoDB is a fully managed, scalable key-value and document database service that uses a distributed architecture to provide high availability and fault tolerance. It uses concepts like **consistent hashing** and **quorum-based approaches** to manage data across a large number of nodes.

- **Consistent Hashing**: DynamoDB uses consistent hashing to distribute data across multiple nodes, ensuring that when nodes are added or removed, minimal data needs to be relocated.

- **Quorum-based Reads and Writes**: DynamoDB uses a quorum-based approach for **eventual consistency**, allowing it to achieve high availability while ensuring that data is eventually consistent across all nodes.

2. Google Bigtable

Google Bigtable is a distributed, scalable storage system designed to handle large amounts of structured data across many servers. It is used in various Google products like **Google Search**, **Gmail**, and **Google Maps**.

288

- **Data Partitioning**: Bigtable partitions data into tablets, and each tablet is stored on a separate machine. Tablets are distributed using **consistent hashing**.
- **Replication**: Bigtable replicates data across multiple servers for fault tolerance, and it uses **quorum-based approaches** to ensure that reads and writes are consistent.

3. Apache Cassandra

Apache Cassandra is an open-source, highly scalable NoSQL database designed to handle large amounts of data across multiple commodity servers without a single point of failure. It combines **DHT** and **quorum-based replication** to ensure that data is distributed across multiple nodes for scalability and reliability.

- **DHT and Consistent Hashing**: Cassandra uses **consistent hashing** for data distribution, allowing it to scale horizontally.
- **Quorum-Based Consistency**: Cassandra provides tunable consistency levels, allowing users to configure the number of replicas that need to acknowledge a write or read operation.

Conclusion

In this chapter, we explored **distributed data structures** and their role in building **resilient and scalable systems**. We discussed:

- **Key techniques** like **consistent hashing, distributed hash tables**, and **quorum-based approaches** that enable distributed systems to scale while maintaining high availability and fault tolerance.

- **Real-world applications** in **distributed storage systems** such as **Amazon DynamoDB, Google Bigtable**, and **Apache Cassandra**, where these distributed data structures are used to efficiently manage large volumes of data.

Distributed data structures are crucial for developing modern distributed systems, and understanding their principles allows developers to design systems that are both scalable and resilient to failure. In the next chapter, we will explore **advanced distributed algorithms**, including **consensus protocols** and **replication strategies**, which are essential for ensuring consistency and fault tolerance in large-scale distributed systems.

CHAPTER 27

THE FUTURE OF DATA STRUCTURES AND ALGORITHMS

As we move further into the 21st century, the landscape of computing is undergoing rapid transformation, driven by **emerging technologies** such as **quantum computing, artificial intelligence (AI), blockchain**, and **machine learning (ML)**. These advancements are not only changing how we approach computing problems, but they are also shaping the future of **data structures** and **algorithms**. The evolution of these fields promises to open up new possibilities for handling vast amounts of data, improving computational efficiency, and solving problems previously deemed intractable.

In this chapter, we will:

- Explore **evolving trends** in data structures, including the impact of **quantum computing** and **AI-based data management**.
- Discuss **anticipated advancements** in **algorithms** and **computational theory**.

- Examine how **emerging technologies** like **blockchain** and **machine learning** will influence the future of **data structures** and algorithms.

Evolving Trends in Data Structures

1. Quantum Computing and Its Impact on Data Structures

Quantum computing represents a fundamental shift in computing, utilizing principles of quantum mechanics to process information in ways that traditional computers cannot. Quantum computers leverage **quantum bits (qubits)**, which can exist in multiple states simultaneously (superposition), and can be entangled, allowing for the potential to perform complex computations exponentially faster than classical computers.

Impact on Data Structures:

- **Quantum data structures** are still in their infancy, but researchers are exploring how quantum computers can be used to enhance data structures. For instance, **quantum-linked lists**, **quantum trees**, and **quantum search algorithms** could outperform classical counterparts in terms of speed and efficiency.
- Quantum **hashing** and **sorting** algorithms are expected to benefit from quantum algorithms like **Grover's search**

algorithm, which provides a quadratic speedup over classical search algorithms.

- **Quantum databases**: There is also ongoing research in **quantum database management systems** (QDMS), which may use quantum data structures to enable faster and more efficient querying of large datasets.

Challenges:

- **Error correction** in quantum data structures will be a significant challenge due to the inherently unstable nature of qubits.
- The development of practical, scalable quantum data structures and algorithms will require breakthroughs in quantum hardware and theory.

2. AI-Based Data Management

Artificial Intelligence is revolutionizing how we handle, process, and manage data. Traditional data structures and algorithms are often not well-suited for handling the dynamic, unstructured data types produced by AI systems, such as **images**, **text**, and **sensor data**.

Impact on Data Structures:

- **AI-powered data structures** are emerging, such as self-optimizing or **adaptive data structures** that can change their configuration based on usage patterns and workload predictions.

- **Neural networks** and **deep learning** models, which involve large, multi-dimensional arrays of data, require new ways of efficiently managing and accessing data. Techniques like **tensor data structures** are becoming more prominent, enabling efficient computation on multi-dimensional arrays used in machine learning.

- **Reinforcement learning** algorithms may be used to dynamically adjust data structures in response to changing conditions, leading to more **intelligent storage systems**.

Future Considerations:

- The growing use of AI in data management will likely lead to more **autonomous systems** that can self-organize, optimize, and maintain their own data structures without manual intervention.

- **Explainable AI (XAI)** and **data transparency** will push the development of data structures that make the internal workings of AI models more interpretable and understandable.

Anticipated Advancements in Algorithms and Computational Theory

1. Evolution of Computational Theory

The theoretical foundations of algorithms and computational complexity are being challenged by new paradigms such as quantum computing and **distributed systems**. Future advancements in computational theory could redefine what is computationally feasible, changing the very limits of what algorithms can achieve.

Key Trends in Computational Theory:

- **Quantum Algorithms**: Quantum computing will enable algorithms that are fundamentally faster than their classical counterparts, challenging the limitations of classical computational theory.
- **Post-Quantum Cryptography**: With the advent of quantum computers, the need for new **cryptographic algorithms** to secure data will lead to the development of **quantum-resistant algorithms**. This will have implications for data structures, especially in the context of secure data storage and transmission.
- **Distributed Algorithms**: As cloud and edge computing systems become more pervasive, algorithms for managing data in highly distributed environments will

295

evolve. Future distributed algorithms will need to account for challenges like **latency**, **fault tolerance**, and **data consistency** in real-time systems.

2. Algorithmic Complexity in the Age of Big Data

As the volume of data continues to grow exponentially, algorithms will need to become more efficient at processing, querying, and analyzing massive datasets. **Big data** algorithms will evolve to handle increasingly complex, heterogeneous, and unstructured data.

- **Approximation Algorithms**: In the face of huge datasets, exact solutions may no longer be feasible. **Approximation algorithms** will play an increasingly important role in finding near-optimal solutions in polynomial time for problems that were previously NP-hard.
- **Parallel and Distributed Algorithms**: Future algorithms will heavily rely on parallel and distributed computing to process data faster. Advances in **GPU computing**, **cloud-based computing**, and **edge computing** will enable algorithms to process vast amounts of data in parallel.
- **Streaming Algorithms**: With data constantly flowing from IoT devices and sensors, new algorithms for processing **data streams** in real time will become more critical. These algorithms must be **memory-efficient** and

capable of providing insights without storing entire datasets.

How Emerging Technologies Like Blockchain and Machine Learning Will Impact Data Structures

1. Blockchain Technology

Blockchain technology, which underpins cryptocurrencies like Bitcoin, is a decentralized, distributed ledger that records transactions across a network of computers. Blockchain has the potential to transform data structures by enabling secure, tamper-resistant data management systems.

Impact on Data Structures:

- **Immutable Data Structures**: Blockchain's inherent property of immutability will lead to the development of **tamper-proof data structures** for secure storage of sensitive information. These structures will be used for storing medical records, financial data, and digital assets.
- **Distributed Ledgers and Consensus Algorithms**: Data structures such as **Merkle trees** and **hash trees** will become more widely used to maintain the integrity of distributed ledgers in blockchain systems. Consensus

297

algorithms, like **Proof of Work** and **Proof of Stake**, will continue to drive innovations in distributed data management.

- **Smart Contracts**: As blockchain integrates with **smart contracts**, which automatically execute when certain conditions are met, specialized data structures for securely storing contract data and ensuring contract integrity will become increasingly important.

Future Applications:

- Blockchain and distributed ledgers could create **decentralized databases** where data is stored across multiple nodes with cryptographic guarantees of security, privacy, and availability.
- **Data provenance** will be revolutionized as blockchain allows tracking of the entire lifecycle of data, ensuring transparency and security.

2. Machine Learning (ML) and Data Structures

Machine learning is a rapidly advancing field that deals with algorithms and models that enable computers to learn from and make decisions based on data. As machine learning becomes more integrated into everyday applications, it will have a profound impact on data structures and algorithms.

298

Impact on Data Structures:

- **Efficient Storage for Training Data**: As datasets used in machine learning grow larger, data structures that can efficiently store and retrieve training data are becoming essential. **Sparse matrices, tensor data structures**, and **graph-based data structures** will become increasingly important in ML applications.

- **Data Preprocessing**: Data preprocessing and feature extraction are critical steps in ML workflows. New data structures will be developed to efficiently handle data transformations, especially when working with heterogeneous data sources (e.g., text, images, and time series data).

- **Memory Efficiency**: Machine learning models, especially deep learning models, require large amounts of memory and computational resources. New data structures will emerge to store and process weights and activations efficiently, especially in **neural networks** and **deep learning** frameworks.

Future Applications:

- Data structures will evolve to better support **recurrent neural networks (RNNs)**, **convolutional neural networks (CNNs)**, and **transformers** by providing optimized storage and retrieval of multi-dimensional data.

299

- **Reinforcement learning** and **decision-making algorithms** will require data structures that can efficiently store and update state-action values, policies, and reward signals.

Conclusion

In this chapter, we explored the **future of data structures and algorithms**, focusing on how emerging technologies like **quantum computing, AI, blockchain**, and **machine learning** are shaping the landscape of computational theory and data management. We discussed:

- The role of **quantum computing** and **AI-based data management** in the evolution of data structures.
- The future advancements in **algorithms** for big data, streaming data, and distributed systems.
- How **blockchain** and **machine learning** are influencing the design of new, efficient data structures.

As technology continues to advance, the future of data structures will be driven by the need for **resilience, scalability**, and **efficiency** in handling increasingly complex, large-scale data. Understanding these emerging trends will be crucial for anyone working in fields like **data science, software engineering**, and

distributed systems, where the demand for innovative data management solutions will only grow.

www.ingramcontent.com/pod-product-compliance
Lightning Source LLC
LaVergne TN
LVHW051434050326
832903LV00030BD/3081